The Kingdom of
BENIN
in West Africa

*F*or their generous assistance and expert advice, the author wishes to thank
Clarence G. Seckel, Jr., Curriculum Coordinator in the Social Studies,
East Saint Louis School District 189, East Saint Louis, Illinois;
Dr. Kate Ezra, Professor of Art History, Columbia College, Chicago, Illinois; and
Dr. Ademola Iyi-Eweka, Research Fellow at the University of Wisconsin at Madison
and Prince of the Kingdom of Benin.

CULTURES OF THE PAST

THE KINGDOM OF
BENIN
IN WEST AFRICA

HEATHER MILLAR

BENCHMARK BOOKS

MARSHALL CAVENDISH
NEW YORK

Benchmark Books
Marshall Cavendish Corporation
99 White Plains Road
Tarrytown, New York 10591-9001

© Marshall Cavendish Corporation 1997

Library of Congress Cataloging-in-Publication Data
Millar, Heather, date.
    The kingdom of Benin in West Africa / by Heather Millar.
       p.   cm. — (Cultures of the past)
    Includes bibliographical references and index.
    Summary: Presents the history and culture of the kingdom which 500 years
ago outshone all others on Africa's west coast and which is now part of Nigeria.
    ISBN 0-7614-0088-5 (lib. bdg.)
    1. Bini (African people)—History—Juvenile literature. 2. Bini (African
people)—Social life and customs—Juvenile literature. 3. Benin (Nigeria)—
History—Juvenile literature. 4. Benin (Nigeria)—Social life and customs—
Juvenile literature.   [1. Bini (African people) 2. Benin (Nigeria)]   I. Title.
II. Series.
DT515.45.B56M55   1997
966.9'32—dc20   95-44098

Printed in Hong Kong

Book design by Carol Matsuyama
Photo research by Ede Rothaus

Front cover: A brass plaque that was made in the early seventeenth century to decorate
    the Royal Palace of Benin. It depicts the slaughter of a cow, probably during a
    ceremony.
Back cover: A modern-day Edo woman and her daughter sit before a shrine to Olokun,
    guardian of pregnancy and childbirth.

Photo Credits
Front cover: courtesy of Werner Forman Archive/British Museum, London/Art
Resource, NY; back cover: courtesy of ©Phyllis Galembo; page 6: Werner Forman/Art
Resource, NY; pages 7, 20, 22, 29, 38, 48, 49: The Metropolitan Museum of Art,
1991; pages 8, 24, 26, 28, 47, 51: The Metropolitan Museum of Art, Gift of Mr. and
Mrs. Klaus G. Perls, 1991; pages 9, 25, 31, 32, 34, 35, 46, 50, 53, 59: ©André Held;
pages 13, 15, 21, 42: Werner Forman Archive/British Museum, London/Art Resource,
NY; page 19: ©Angela Fisher/Robert Estall Photo Agency; pages 23, 39, 63, 66, 68,
69, 70, 72: ©Phyllis Galembo; pages 41, 44, 71: ©Norma Rosen; page 56: Aldo
Tutino/Art Resource, NY; page 60: ©Joseph Nevadomsky, 1986; pages 61, 64: ©James
H. Morris/Panos Pictures

CONTENTS

CHAPTER ONE

BENIN: A STORY OF GLORY AND SUFFERING

The people of Benin were highly skilled brass sculptors. This brass plaque, which depicts three warriors and their attendants, was made in the 1700s to decorate the palace of the obas.

Five hundred years ago, the kingdom of Benin (buh-NEEN) outshone all others on the west coast of Africa. At no time did the kingdom glitter more than when a new king was about to be crowned. The people of Benin called their king the *oba* (OH-bah). They believed that he was a demigod—part god, part man. His ancestors were said to have been gods. The well-being of the entire kingdom depended on him. So when a new *oba* came to the throne, his subjects spared no expense to put on the grandest spectacle ever. Few written records of the coronation ceremonies exist, but it is likely that the crowning of a great *oba* called Ozolua (oh-zo-LOO-a) happened in this way:

For seven days before his coronation in about 1481 C.E.,* the crown prince stayed in a special camp in Benin City, the capital. There, he cleansed himself and prepared himself spiritually for the great responsibility of becoming *oba*. Meanwhile, the kingdom feverishly got ready. People from the great sandy plains and the rain forest, people from all over the 250-mile (402-kilometer)-wide realm, sent gifts: baskets of yams, palm wine, cloth, elephant tusks, and bars of brass, a metal considered more precious than gold. Within the tall city walls,

*Many systems of dating have been used by different cultures throughout history. This series of books uses B.C.E. (Before Common Era) and C.E. (Common Era) instead of B.C. (Before Christ) and A.D. (Anno Domini) out of respect for the diversity of the world's peoples.

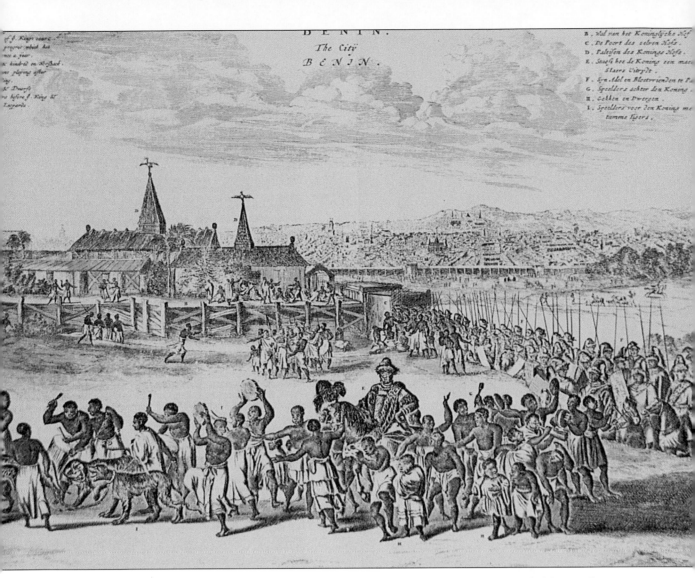

Surrounded by acrobats, attendants, and tame leopards, the oba *makes a rare, grand procession among his people. His chiefs, on horseback, and warriors follow behind. In the distance lies the walled city of Benin. Nearby stands a walled compound enclosing the royal palace. A European visitor engraved this picture in the 1600s.*

along the 100-foot (30.5-meter)-wide avenues, hundreds of crafts-people prepared the treasures that would be used in the ceremony: brass swords of state that shimmered red-gold in the sun, red cloth for the nobles, special beads and jewelry for the royal family.

On the day of the coronation, the crown prince made a grand procession to Use (ooh-SAY), a special village outside the capi-tal. This was a rare event. Normally, the *oba* did not show himself to his people; he was too sacred. But on this day, the crown prince rode on one of his best horses, which was decorated with bells. Young men ran down the streets ahead of him, blowing trumpets with deep, piercing tones. Then came three or four hundred nobles, or chiefs, wearing red robes and brass ornaments. Around the crown prince, acrobats did flips and cartwheels. Musicians in

7

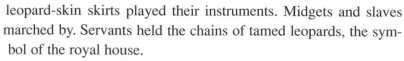

leopard-skin skirts played their instruments. Midgets and slaves marched by. Servants held the chains of tamed leopards, the symbol of the royal house.

The procession stopped briefly at the village where the kingdom's first *oba* had grown up. Here, the crown prince chose his ruling title: Ozolua. Then he and all his attendants continued to the ancient palace first built for his ancestors, who were believed to be gods. There, the crown prince went through complicated ceremonies. He symbolically bought the land of Benin from some of his chiefs, who represented the people. Leopards and slaves were killed in his honor and offered to the gods. For the first time, he put on the royal crown and royal robes made of red coral beads.

When Ozolua returned to Benin City and the royal palace there, he was no longer just a man. He had become divine. No ordinary mortal dared to look him in the face as his procession went by. He now held the power of life and death over all the people, and the fate of the kingdom lay in his hands.

A Grand Tradition

The details of Ozolua's coronation ceremonies had evolved over centuries. The people of Benin, who called themselves the Edo (eh-DOE) or the Bini (BEE-nee), didn't write down their traditions. They passed them on by word of mouth for hundreds of years, using their language, also called Edo. Their history was not recorded until European visitors began to write about Benin in the late fifteenth century. Thus, the dates of their history prior to 1500 are approximate.

According to their oral tradition, the Edo people first settled on the west coast of Africa about 900 C.E. They built high earthen walls around their villages. As the villages grew and the boundaries increased, so did the walls.

This brass statue, made in Benin in the twentieth century, shows the oba *wearing a royal costume probably identical to the one that Ozolua would have worn at his coronation five hundred years earlier. His crown has spiky projections that reach heavenward, showing the* oba's *connection to the gods.*

Eventually, they formed an enormous complex web, hundreds of miles long.

After a while, one of the village leaders dominated the others. He took the title of *ogiso* (oh-gee-SO), which means "ruler of the sky." Despite his powerful-sounding name, the *ogiso* ruled with the consent of other chiefs. The title of *ogiso* was passed down from son to son. Tradition says that thirty-one *ogisos* ruled, but many of their names have been lost, and no one is really sure. Even so, the *ogisos* are credited with introducing the royal throne and the swords of authority, as well as domestic tools like round leather fans, wooden plates, and mortars for grinding grain and spices.

The leopard, the strongest wild cat in the forest, was a symbol of the oba's *power. An Edo artist crafted this one in bronze during the height of the kingdom's power.*

The last *ogiso,* named Owodo (oh-woe-DOE), got into trouble because he could not have children. Only one of his wives had had a son, and his senior wife, who was jealous, had tricked him into banishing the young man. Finally, Owodo realized his mistake and asked his son to return, but he refused. Time passed, and still none of his other wives bore children. Perhaps this made Owodo crazy, because gradually he started to rule very badly. When he ordered the execution of a pregnant woman, the people rose up in anger. They banished Owodo, as he had banished his son, and the childless ruler died miserably in a small distant village.

Now the Edo had no king. They turned to a man named Evian (ay-vee-AN), who was well respected because he had killed a monster that had been attacking the central market. Evian ran the government for several years. But when old age eventually caught up with him, Evian proposed that his son take over. The people resisted this idea. They said that Evian's son wasn't really an *ogiso.* Everyone started arguing about what to do.

The Test of the Seven Lice

Finally the people sent a messenger to the nearby kingdom of Ife (EE-fay). The messenger went to the king there, called the *oni* (AW-nee). He asked the *oni* to send one of his sons to be their ruler before things in Benin went from bad to worse. The *oni* of Ife considered this request, and then said that he would give the Edo a test before he decided.

The *oni* sent the messenger back to Benin with seven lice, small white insect pests that live in human hair and animal fur. He told the Edo to care for the pests and return them in three years. The chiefs obeyed, and put the lice in the hair of their slaves. After three years had gone by, the chiefs returned the lice, healthy and much fatter than they had been when they arrived. The *oni* of Ife was pleased. He said that any people that could take such good care of common pests could certainly take care of his son.

Around 1200 the *oni* sent his son Oranmiyan (oh-ran-ME-yan) to be the ruler of Benin. Oranmiyan set up his household in a palace the people had built for him. He married an Edo woman, and together they had a son. After several years in his new country, Oranmiyan got very frustrated. He couldn't understand the Edo language and Edo ways of doing things. He finally decided that only someone raised in Benin from birth could rule over the Edo people. He gave up his throne and went home to Ife, leaving his son in the care of elders at the village of Use, not far from Benin City.

A Rule of *Obas*

Around 1300 C.E., that son became Eweka (ay-way-KAH), the first *oba* of Benin. Unlike the *ogisos,* who had ruled as a group, the *oba* was considered the supreme ruler. Tradition remembers Eweka's reign as "long and glorious," but not many details survive. At first the fact that the *oba* was of foreign ancestry increased the power and mystery of the ruler. But as he became stronger, the *oba* came into conflict with the chiefs. During the next two hundred years or so, the *obas* steadily gained more and more control. They introduced rules that highlighted their superiority and gave them more power over their chiefs.

Oba Ewuare (eh-woo-ARE-ay) put on the coral crown about

1440 C.E. After the original palace in Benin City was destroyed during a dispute with his brother, Ewuare built a new palace, widened the city streets, and surrounded it all with a new defensive wall and a moat. During his long reign he introduced sweeping changes in the government, creating a new category of "town chiefs," comparable to modern governors. He traveled widely, conquering two hundred towns and adding them to the Benin empire. He is remembered as Ewuare the Great.

Shortly after Ewuare died, about 1481 C.E., Ozolua came to the throne. The kingdom expanded in all directions during his reign. He waged war upon a different town every six months or so. After a victory he sent off one of his sons to rule the new areas and spread the idea of divine kingship. He became known as Ozolua the Conqueror and the kingdom grew rich under him. This was not only because conquered villages sent taxes and tribute to the palace. It was also because traders from Portugal appeared on the Benin coast during his reign, in 1486 C.E.

The Europeans first came in search of a shorter route to India, where they bought spices like pepper and cinnamon. But they found Benin a great source for pepper, as well as for cotton cloth, ivory, and slaves, so they kept coming back. They paid for Edo products with European cloth, coral beads, and brass rings. The Edo used the brass and coral to make religious statues and jewelry. As the trade continued, the kingdom of Benin grew even more wealthy and sophisticated. Some Edo princes learned to read, write, and speak Portuguese. When Portugal's king sent a representative to Benin, the *oba* returned the honor by sending Edo princes to Portugal. Not long after the arrival of the Portuguese, around 1516, Christian missionaries also came to Benin.

Benin's Golden Age

The next hundred years or so were the period of Benin's greatest glory. At this time Europe and Africa compared equally in technology. European visitors to Benin were impressed by the size of the Edo capital. They wrote that the streets of Benin City were longer and wider than those in most European cities. They described the *oba*'s palace as the grandest in West Africa, with large apartments

BENIN'S ROLE IN THE SLAVE TRADE

Unfortunate people labored as slaves in Africa long before Europeans came to the continent. Usually, African slaves were prisoners of war or criminals who had been sentenced to slavery as punishment. In Benin, as in ancient Rome, one of the main ways the ruler and nobles grew rich was by amassing large numbers of slaves who could work on their farms for them.

Small groups of African slaves also made their way overseas. During the days of ancient Egypt, Greece, and Rome, some Africans were sold northward down the Nile, or across the Sahara Desert. A few ended up in Mediterranean cities. Trade in slaves continued for thousands of years in North and East Africa, and was especially important to the economies of the ancient Egyptians and the medieval Muslims.

There was nothing like a "slave trade," however, until the seventeenth century C.E., when European traders showed up on the west coast of Africa. At the same time, North and South America were being settled by Europeans. Settlers in the Americas needed laborers for their farms and plantations. This demand fueled the trade in slaves. Ships transported millions from Africa, across the Atlantic to the Americas.

Lured by the wealth the Europeans offered for slaves, some African rulers started to punish even minor crimes by selling the accused. Others declared wars so that they could sell the prisoners that a war would create. Many conducted raids on neighboring kingdoms for the sole purpose of capturing slaves to sell.

Recent studies estimate that between fifteen million and twenty million Africans were taken to the Americas on slave ships. Of these as many as ten million came from the Guinea coast, where Benin is located. The majority of African-Americans trace their roots back to this part of Africa, as do many blacks in Brazil and Spain's former colonies.

At first, Benin's *obas* forbade the export of male slaves, who were needed to maintain the kingdom's strength. But gradually, Benin was drawn into the slave trade. Of course, the *oba* controlled the export of captives. Some of them were Edo, but most were prisoners of war from nearby kingdoms like Yorubaland. In return for slaves the Europeans paid the *oba* with highly valued brass, coral beads, European cloth, guns, rum, and tobacco. A healthy young man or woman was worth the equivalent of about three British pounds in the late seventeenth century. By the dawn of the nineteenth century, the price had risen to the equivalent of twenty-seven British pounds.

While African kings profited from the slave trade, many scholars believe that the trade eventually hurt their kingdoms. It drained healthy young people who could have helped build African societies and no doubt created an atmosphere of fear. Of course it was miserable for the slaves themselves.

After the original royal palace was destroyed in war, Oba Ewuare rebuilt the palace, the outer walls of which are still visible today. During the fifteenth and sixteenth centuries, the obas *made the palace grander than ever before. They filled its rooms and halls with shining brass ornaments like this plaque, which shows the* oba's *butchers slaughtering a cow.*

linked by rows of columns decorated with brass plaques depicting military victories and religious pageants.

Ozolua was followed by a series of *obas* who made further conquests for Benin and added to the grandeur of the capital. Benin was securely situated. The central part of the kingdom was surrounded by a thick jungle of rain forest. Neighboring kingdoms posed little threat in any case. The *oba* maintained an enormous army: at least thirty thousand men, sometimes as many as one hundred thousand. At that time it was the largest military force in West Africa.

People in other kingdoms trembled when they heard Benin was on the march. The Edo army made human sacrifices to the god of death before they went to war, and again when they came back in victory. People called Edo soldiers the Children of Death. Legend has it that people deserted their villages and ran into the bush when they heard the bells and drums of the Edo army approaching. Armed with spears, poisoned arrows, javelins, and swords, Edo chiefs and their soldiers ruled absolutely in an area smaller than most states in the United States, about 400 miles (644 kilometers) across. But the *oba*'s word was respected over a much larger region.

The Kingdom Declines

During the seventeenth century, Benin society began to decline. Arguments about who was to be the next king divided the country. Several bitter civil wars broke out. None of the seven *obas* who ruled during this time did anything notable, except to waste the kingdom's riches and anger the chiefs.

A Brief Rebirth of Glory

At the beginning of the eighteenth century, Oba Ewuakpe (AA-woo-AHK-pay) came to the throne. Though his early reign was very difficult, he managed to restore the power of the *oba* and the fortunes of the kingdom. His son, Akenzua (ah-ken-ZOO-ah), benefited from a revival of trade with Europeans, this time with the Dutch. He became one of the wealthiest *obas* ever to rule, and so did his son. Stories about Akenzua's son, Eresonyen (air-SON-yen), are still told: He had so many cowrie shells, used as money

In times of strength the armies of Benin were the terror of West Africa. This brass palace plaque features a chief in the ceremonial dress of a warrior. He wears a necklace of teeth from the powerful leopard, and his tunic is decorated with a leopard's head. Edo warriors hoped to be as terrifying to their enemies as the leopard is to its prey.

15

by the Edo, that he built a house and covered its floors and walls with the precious shells. Brass, that highly valued metal, "fell from the sky" during his reign.

Although the authority of the *obas* had been restored, this situation was only temporary. The kingdom's power began to weaken from the late eighteenth century and into the nineteenth century. Civil wars—probably caused by fights over succession—damaged the country's prosperity. The *obas* retreated into their palaces; it was no longer safe to leave the capital for extended periods because rebellious chiefs might try to take over the government. Some chiefs refused to pay taxes to the *oba*. Revolts became common. European trade with Benin's vassals, however, continued to flourish. Unfortunately this trade would eventually cause the near destruction of the kingdom.

The Beginning of the End

In late 1896 a British official named James Phillips decided that he wanted to visit the current ruler of Benin, Oba Ovonrramwen (OH-voo-rah-MAY). He wanted to complain that the *oba* had not kept his part of a trading agreement made a few years earlier. Oba Ovonrramwen sent word that it was not a good time. Important rituals were being performed, and the ruler could not meet with him. Phillips paid no attention to the *oba*'s message. Instead he got together 8 other Europeans and 240 Africans to carry supplies and gifts for the *oba*. The group packed their guns away to show they were coming in peace. When they were in thick forest a few miles from Benin City, they were ambushed. Edo warriors attacked them, killing almost everyone. Only two of the Europeans escaped.

It seems that the *oba* did not order the attack, and that it was carried out by a group of chiefs. This fact did not soften the anger of the British when news of the incident reached London. Newspaper headlines in London screamed that Benin was a "city of blood." In part, the British made such a big deal of the raid because they wanted an excuse to invade. Benin and the *oba* were the last African obstacles to a British colony in the Niger River area. The *oba* surely knew that the British would strike back because of the Edo raid.

Other powerful African kingdoms near Benin had already been defeated by the British. But the Edo kept hoping that the *oba*'s godlike powers would save them. They didn't.

Several weeks after the raid, in early 1897, a British force of fifteen hundred soldiers marched on Benin City and captured it. In what became known as the British Punitive Expedition, they blew up sections of the city. Fires destroyed a large part of the rest. British troops broke into the *oba*'s sacred palace. They stole all the *oba*'s precious art and treasure and shipped it back to London. Benin's treasure was sold to art dealers to pay the cost of the expedition.

Oba Ovonrramwen, the man who was a demigod, was forced to rub his head on the ground three times in front of the British and a large crowd of Edo people. The British put the *oba* and his chiefs on trial. They executed two chiefs and banished the *oba* from Benin for the rest of his life. It seemed that the great kingdom had ceased to exist. Benin had become part of the British Empire.

Modern Benin

In time the British made changes in their colonial policies. They decided they could better control their empire by allowing native kings to rule. In 1914 the British governor of the colony of Nigeria crowned the eldest son of the deposed *oba* and restored the royal coral beads to him.

The new *oba* of Benin took the title of the very first *oba*: Eweka. Calling himself Eweka II, he said he was starting a new era for Benin. He rebuilt the palace and restored the titles of the chiefs. He ordered artists to make brass and ivory objects to begin replacing the ones stolen by the British. He restored the royal altars and began to perform state rituals again. His son, Akenzua II, who was crowned in 1933, continued these efforts.

Today Eweka II's grandson rules Benin, now part of the independent nation of Nigeria. The current *oba*'s name is Erediauwa (AA-ray-DEE-ow-wah). Though he wears modern eyeglasses, he carries on traditions that are at least eight hundred years old. Benin was the first kingdom to rise in the forests of West Africa. It has known both glory and suffering. Many ancient kingdoms, like the

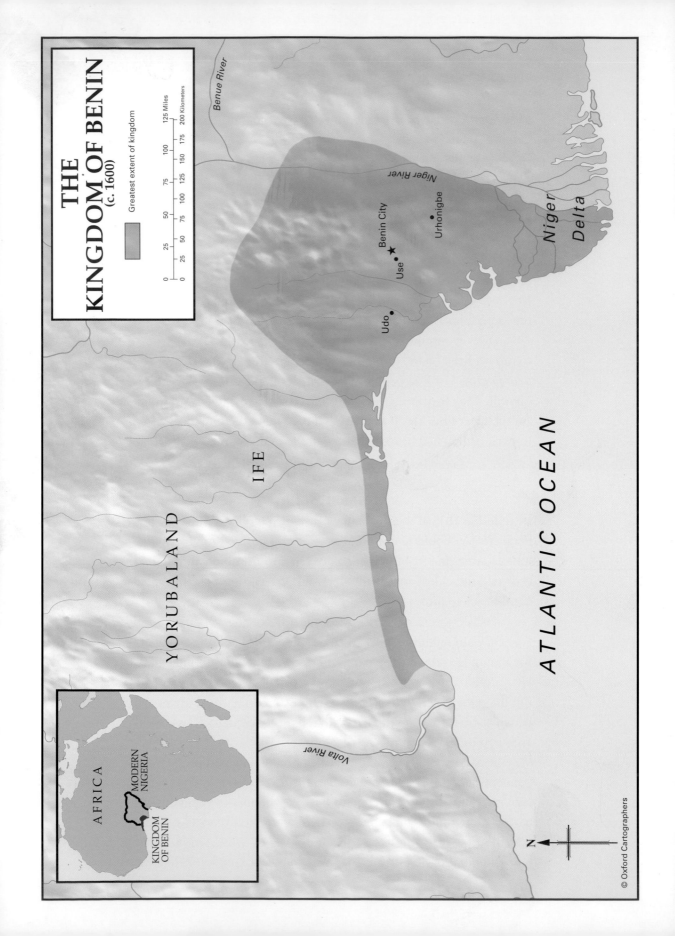

THE KINGDOM OF BENIN
(c. 1600)

Greatest extent of kingdom

125 Miles
200 Kilometers

100
150

75
125

50
100

75

25
50

25

0
0

Benue River

Niger River

Niger

Delta

Urhonigbe

Benin City

Use

Udo

IFE

YORUBALAND

ATLANTIC OCEAN

Volta River

AFRICA

MODERN NIGERIA

KINGDOM OF BENIN

N

© Oxford Cartographers

Incas of Peru and the Aztecs of Mexico, have disappeared, leaving only impressive stone ruins. Some great civilizations, like those of Greece and China, have survived, but have changed so much that their founders would hardly recognize them. Benin, however, has endured: The culture, art, and government of centuries past survive to this day.

Today's Oba Erediauwa wears modern eyeglasses as he participates in an ancient ritual to honor his dead ancestors. The oba *wears the same royal costume depicted in brass statues hundreds of years old. Note the ruler's coral-bead crown, coral collar and necklaces, belt of coral beads, "wrapper" of coral-bead netting, and ivory masks at the waist.*

19

CHAPTER TWO

KINGDOM OF BRASS AND IVORY

This ivory mask shows the face of the oba's *mother, or queen mother. During ceremonies honoring his mother, the* oba *probably wore the mask suspended from a necklace or attached to his hip or waist.*

Benin's culture—its art, music, stories, and ways of doing things—revolved mainly around the king. Not only was the *oba* their ruler, but he was believed to have control over the conditions that made a harvest plentiful or foreign trade profitable. "The *oba* is the center of prosperity," people said. Images of the *oba* abounded. Metal sculptors created beautiful brass statues of the king, his family, and important chiefs. Artists carved images of the *oba*'s court on long elephant tusks and broad pieces of fine wood. Dancers and musicians gave special performances for the *oba* and his court. The *oba* himself played a central role in most of the rituals that punctuated the Edo year.

Life on a Grand Scale

Benin City, where the *oba* made his home, was an impressive capital. A wall ten feet (three meters) high surrounded it, forming a rough circle six miles (ten kilometers) around. Travelers approaching the city from the sandy coastal marshes or from the inland rain forests would first see the wall. Above it, they would see the tall, pointed towers of the city within. Enormous brass birds perched on the tops of the towers. A huge, brass snake slithered down one tower, beginning sixty or seventy feet (eighteen or twenty-one meters) up. The snake tower stood in the *oba*'s palace, and represented his wealth. "Like the viper who waits for his prey, the *oba* waits for the people's tribute," the saying went.

If the travelers were just visiting Benin City, they were likely to be bringing tribute to the *oba* or coming to trade. Like all capital cities, Benin City required an enormous amount of trade and tribute, or taxes, to keep it up. Thousands of buildings stood within the city walls. Made of mud brick and roofed with tightly

The oba *was central to the culture of Benin. This brass plaque depicts the imposing entrance to the* oba's *palace. Soldiers, with shields, and two attendants flank the doorway. The serpent above the doorway represents the* oba's *wealth and power.*

In this bronze statuette a court official wears the ornaments befitting his high rank: coral necklaces, a shallow-brimmed hat, and a tunic of coral beadwork.

woven grasses and twigs, these buildings housed thousands upon thousands of people: government officials, craftsmen, priests, servants, court ladies, powerful chiefs. Most Edo were farmers, but few, if any, of these city dwellers tilled the land. They all depended on trade and tribute to live.

Of course the largest household was the *oba*'s. His palace had hundreds of rooms. Music and dancing filled its chambers. In the halls, ministers schemed to get more power for themselves. The *oba*'s special servants, who were given to him as babies, rushed around delivering messages and doing the king's errands. A dizzying number of officials went about their jobs: the master of the *oba*'s wardrobe, the recorder of deaths, the keepers of the *oba*'s harem, and on and on. The *oba* had hundreds of wives and children who lived in the harem, located in a special part of the palace. Only one entrance led to the harem, and guards watched over it.

Dressing in Royal Finery

It is hot most of the year in Benin, so the clothes people wore seem simple by modern standards. The women wrapped large pieces of cloth around themselves, the way people today might wrap themselves in a towel after a shower. The men wore smaller pieces of cloth that looked somewhat like modern skirts. These clothes were airy and cool. The *oba*'s courtiers wore cloth of the finest cotton, woven with patterns representing the *oba* and certain sacred objects. For special occasions, the chiefs wore a special red flannel called *ododo* (oh-DOE-doe).

To an Edo the most obvious signs of wealth and power were a person's coral ornaments and jewelry. Coral feels like a stone, but is actually formed by the hardened skeletons of tiny sea creatures. When taken out of the sea and polished, most coral becomes a shiny reddish pink. It can be cut and shaped into beads and other kinds of finery. The Edo believed that one of the great *obas* had defeated the sea god in a wrestling match and had stolen his coral beads. Therefore all coral was the *oba*'s property. It was sacred beyond price. The only coral found outside the palace came in gifts from the *oba* himself.

The *oba* would give coral to people who pleased him. His wives wore patterns of coral beads in their hair, stringing them into braids and then arranging the braids in small circles. They wore high hairdos held in place with coral-topped pins. The wives almost covered their chests with coral necklaces. The *oba* awarded coral necklaces to his officials. Receiving such a strand of coral was an honor equal to receiving a knighthood in European courts. When a chief was promoted to run a province or district, the *oba* sent special officials to bestow the Honor of Beads. No chief could ever misplace the coral he received in that ceremony. He would be executed if he lost it. No chief dared appear before the *oba* without his coral necklace. After the chief died, his family had to return the coral beads to the *oba*.

In both old and modern Benin, coral ornaments mark out the powerful. This modern chief's wife wears coral necklaces and hair decorations.

A Year of Holidays

The business of Benin City was more than looking grand and receiving tribute, however. The Edo believed that the actions of the *oba* controlled the welfare of the entire kingdom. Each year, the *oba* and his court led a series of sacred rituals. These ceremonies, the people believed, purified the kingdom and renewed the spiritual powers of the king. Many parts of each ceremony acted out religious ideas, past events, or political relationships. So the rituals also played an important role by bringing Edo religion, history, and politics to life. In the course of one year, the *oba* and his court would spend several months participating in these pageants. They were a central part of Edo culture.

A rite called Ugie Erha Oba (oo-gee AIR-ah oh-BAH) was one of the most important of the year. At this time, the *oba* honored his ancestors on his father's side—in other words, all the *obas* who had gone before him. He also emphasized his role as the supreme leader of the royal court and the nation.

The ceremony took several days and had three parts. In the first part the *oba* led the court in recalling all of the past *obas*. After an *oba* died, an altar to his memory and spirit was built in the palace. The current *oba* made offerings at each of these altars. The second part of the ceremony started the next day. All of the *oba*'s chiefs and officials lined up in order of their rank: The most powerful and senior went first; the most junior went last. One by one these nobles paid homage to the *oba*. In return, the *oba* gave them gifts of palm wine and kola nuts, symbols of hospitality.

This group of figures would be placed at the altar of a queen mother. It depicts a queen mother, wearing her high coral crown, with her attendants.

The central ceremony, the most important part of Ugie Erha Oba, took place on the third day. On that day, the *oba* spent several hours getting dressed. First he put on a long cotton skirt, or "wrapper," decorated with pictures of royal leopards and *obas*. Then servants helped him put on another wrapper, made of a net of coral beads. Then he attached a belt of coral beads. Around his neck he wore a coral collar, like a high coral turtleneck. His head supported a coral-bead crown with tall projections. An ivory ornament on his belt and an ivory bracelet completed his attire.

This sacred outfit weighed a lot. Imagine that all your clothes are made of small pebbles woven together, and you get an idea of its weight. No matter how strong he was, the *oba* needed help standing under all that heavy coral. Two attendants held each of the *oba*'s arms to help him walk.

Dressed in all his finery and assisted by his attendants, the *oba* appeared in public. Servants walked in front of him, clearing a path with magical bracelets. Others carried the *oba*'s *ada* (ah-dah), a ceremonial sword that symbolized his power over life and death.

In Benin almost everything stood for something else. Animals and colors, for example, were symbols for ideas or events, just as the bald eagle stands for the United States and lighting candles at Kwanzaa represents the strength of community. The Edo used dozens upon dozens of symbols. Here are a few of the most important ones:

The Leopard: If the Edo had made movies, their favorite would have been *The Leopard King* rather than *The Lion King.* Since they lived far from the plains where lions roam, the Edo worshiped the dominant wild cat of the rain forest: the leopard. This large animal with its spotted coat stood for swift, ferocious power, as well as for wisdom and fairness. The big cat was the symbol of the *oba,* who also had the power of life and death. Given the power to kill by the *oba,* warriors strung leopard teeth around their necks and used leopard patterns on their shields and costumes.

The Elephant: The largest of the animals, the elephant, was seen to possess great strength and wisdom. Since its ivory tusks were so valuable, it also stood for wealth. The chiefs and other headstrong leaders took the elephant as their sign. The symbol of the royal house combined the leopard and the elephant. Edo art often shows elephant trunks ending in human hands holding leaves. This image represents the strengths and accomplishments of the chiefs, as well as the matchless power of the *oba.*

The Mudfish: The mudfish lives a life that is betwixt and between. During the rainy season, it lives in the water. During the summer drought, it can survive on land for short periods. The Edo believed that their *oba,* like the mudfish, could live in two worlds: the world of the living and the spirit world. Thus the mudfish became the *oba*'s special symbol, embroidered on his clothes and cast in brass.

The Bird of Prophecy: In Edo history, a famous sixteenth-century *oba* was leading his army into battle when he heard a bird cry out. The bird predicted, or prophesied, that the *oba*'s army would meet with disaster. The *oba* marched on anyway. Despite the bird's prediction, the Edo army had a great victory. Thus, the "bird of prophecy" came to stand for the *oba*'s ability to overcome fate. Statues of these birds perched on the towers of Benin City and decorated the clappers chiefs played to honor the *oba.*

A bird of prophecy in brass, symbol of the oba's *power*

Musicians blew horns and pounded drums. Women played rattles made of bead nets stretched over gourds. The *oba* walked through all this activity to the altar of his father, where he made sacrifices of palm wine and animals such as goats and chickens. Then the chiefs raised their ceremonial swords, called *eben* (eh-BEN), and danced around the *oba* to the music of the horns and drums. The *oba* then performed a similar dance before the altar of his father. The ritual ended with "Iron," a ceremony in which the chiefs reenacted an ancient challenge to the *oba*'s power, and the *oba* defeated them. By the close of Ugie Erha Oba, the message was clear: The *oba* reigns supreme.

Sacrifices were part of almost every Edo ceremony. The common people made offerings of humble things like yams and palm oil. The oba, *however, sacrificed things that most men could not afford to kill: cows, goats, and sheep. This brass scene shows the* oba *with animals he will sacrifice to the gods.*

Strengthening the *Oba*'s Spiritual Powers

Another major holiday of the Edo year was Igue (EE-goo-AY), when the Edo celebrated the mystical powers of the *oba*. Again, the festival had three parts. The first day, the chiefs greeted the *oba* one by one. On the second day rituals were performed to strengthen the *oba*'s spiritual power. Officials sacrificed a royal leopard and other animals, such as cows and sheep, to honor the *oba*. Then they ground roots, seeds, and leaves into special potions. They applied these mixtures to the *oba*'s body to provide him with physical and spiritual strength.

Four days later all Edo men across the nation would honor their own *igue,* or spiritual strength. On the day after this, children would run from their homes carrying torches to drive evil spirits away. They ran to the edge of the forest and returned bringing *ewere* (AA-WAIR-ray) leaves, or "leaves of joy." In the palace the chiefs presented the *oba* with the leaves of joy. The leaves expressed the hope that the *oba,* his mystical powers renewed, would guide his people through a prosperous year.

Nearly Every Day a Holiday

In addition to these two important festivals, the Edo celebrated all sorts of other holidays and rituals. Isiokuo (ee-she-OH-kwoh) honored the god of iron and war. The *oba*'s warriors paraded through Benin City. Then acrobats, hanging by ropes from trees, performed a midair "dance" to recall a mythical war against the sky. Priests sacrificed humans, usually slaves, as well as cows and other animals. Like many cultures that practiced human sacrifice, the Edo reserved these sacrifices for the most serious ceremonies: those involving war, fertility, or the *oba*. After the harvest the *oba* performed a thanksgiving ritual, Agwe (AH-gway), making offerings of new yams at all the altars in the palace. Then people across the nation offered new yams at their home altars.

At Ugie-ivie (oo-GEE-ee-vay), priests laid out the *oba*'s beads and crown before the altar of Oba Ewuare. Then, to strengthen the magical power of the beads, they sacrificed a man over the royal robes.

Every other year, the Edo celebrated Eghute (egg-HOO-tay), which they believed ensured healthy births around the nation. In the ritual all the women were sent out of Benin City. Then priests and others dressed up like pregnant women, and a man was sacrificed.

Not only did the Edo mark these major holidays, but they also had family rituals as well as ceremonies honoring local and state gods of all kinds. In old Benin, almost every other day was a holiday!

Art for the *Oba*'s Sake

Until modern times most societies created art mainly to honor their gods. Ancient Egyptians carved statues and built temples for their gods. European Christians built soaring cathedrals and filled them with religious paintings, statues, and stained glass. The Maya of Central America built pyramids to honor their gods. In Benin, also, a large part of the people's creativity was employed in producing works of art to honor the *oba* and the gods. The complex rituals the Edo celebrated demanded all sorts of things: statues and carvings for altars; sacred objects to use in ceremonies; special cloth for the *oba*, the chiefs, and the priests; musical compositions and dances for the various pageants. Making all this kept an entire district of Benin City busy.

The *oba* controlled the part of the capital where the craftsmen labored to turn metal, elephant tusks or ivory, wood, and cloth into art. The *oba* also controlled the trade in rare materials. For every

Head of an oba. *After an* oba *died, his son (the new* oba*) ordered a brass head like this one to place at the dead* oba's *altar. Facial features are not the focus of these statues. Instead the trappings of kingship, the coral crown and bead necklaces, dominate.*

elephant killed in Benin, the first ivory tusk to hit the ground went to the *oba*. Likewise the *oba* regulated all the trade in metals and coral. The Edo believed that the things made from these materials were magic. So the *oba*'s command of the materials and the artists was an important source of his power.

The Magic of Brass

Throughout the world today, Benin is famous for the statues that decorated the *oba*'s palace and adorned the royal altars. Most were made of metal: the majority of a mixture of copper and zinc—brass—and the rest of a mixture of copper and tin—bronze. Without running scientific tests, today it is difficult to tell if the objects are brass or bronze. For the sake of simplicity, we'll use *brass* to describe all the metal statues. Brass polishes to a shiny reddish gold. The Edo thought it was beautiful, and a little frightening—both qualities they linked to the *oba*.

Brass was very difficult to obtain in Benin. There were no copper mines in the nearby rain forests. At first the Edo bought it at a high price from traders journeying from Nubia (modern-day Sudan). Later, after the fifteenth century, they traded slaves and spices to Europeans in return for brass. Unlike other peoples, the Edo had little interest in gold. Even the *oba* possessed only a few gold ornaments. In Benin brass was the thing.

Heads above the Crowd

The most sacred brass objects were statues of the *oba*'s head. This was because the Edo believed the head was the source of power, not only for the *oba*, but for ordinary people as well. Tradition also held that the people of Benin had learned brass casting from

This intricately carved elephant tusk probably was placed on an oba's *altar. Ivory was always a sacred material to the people of Benin.*

a brass artist sent by the *oni* of Ife, the same nearby ruler who sent his son to be the first *oba*. In early times it was said that after an *oba* died, the people sent the *oba*'s head to the *oni* of Ife. The *oni* sent back a brass head to Benin City. After many years the Edo asked the *oni* to send someone to teach them brass casting. The *oni* did. After this, with the death of each *oba*, Edo artists fashioned a brass head of him.

The cast heads are not individual portraits of the *obas*. Rather they are images of an ideal, created to emphasize the king's godlike powers. The heads include the coral-bead crown and high collar of the *oba*'s formal royal costume. No one has been able to determine exactly when each head was made. Generally historians have concluded that the earlier heads are more simple and natural-looking. The metal is also thinner in these early examples. As the centuries went by, the kingdom grew richer and brass became

HOW THE EDO MADE THEIR BRASS MASTERPIECES

Pouring melted brass into a mold may sound no more difficult than pouring batter into a muffin tin. Actually, molding brass is a very difficult process. The artists of Benin had to spend years developing the skills to make the brass statues for which they are famous. This is how they did it, using what is now called the lost-wax casting method:

First the Edo artist carved a statue out of wax. He added all the details that he wanted the finished brass statue to have: the contours of the faces, the designs, the textures. When he was happy with the figure, he added long, thin pieces of wax that looked like straws sticking out of the statue.

Then he covered the wax statue and the "straws" with a thin layer of fine clay. He had to be careful to push the clay into all the little crevices and holes of the wax piece. Then he added layer after layer of coarse clay on top of the fine clay and the wax. Next, he baked the clay in an oven so that it hardened. During the baking, the wax melted and drained out, not only from the statue but from the long strawlike projections, too. What was left? A clay mold with clay straws leading into it.

After this the artist melted brass over a very hot fire. Carefully he poured the molten metal through the clay straws into the empty space left by the wax. When the metal had cooled and hardened, the artist chipped away the clay and revealed a bronze figure just like the wax figure that he had carved at the beginning. Finally, he polished the statue with rough leaves.

The resulting figure was completely unique. The artist had to break the mold to get at the statue. Therefore, there could never be another one exactly like it.

more plentiful. The later heads became thicker, more elaborate and stylized.

After the sixteenth century the artists also began to fashion heads of the *oba*'s mother, the queen mother. She had her own palace and played an important role in the royal court. The brass statues show her wearing a crown with a forward-pointing peak that represents a high "chicken's beak" hairdo. Since only the *oba* and the *oba*'s principal war chiefs normally wore crowns, the crowns on the queen-mother figures show how important she was. The Edo believed that she could use supernatural powers to help her son.

Other Treasures

In addition to head portraits, the brass casters of Benin made many other objects. They crafted ceremonial swords and long staffs that rattled and summoned the spirits. They made brass bells and figurines of royal leopards and warriors. In the sixteenth and seventeenth centuries, they made hundreds of plaques, or rectangular brass pieces, that showed Edo festivals and historical events.

In districts separated from the street of brass casters, other artists worked busily. A street of weavers created cotton cloth with pictures woven into it for chiefs to wear during ceremonies. They also made the chiefs' "hands of wealth," big hand cutouts made of cloth. Carvers crafted rattles, drums, and elephant-tusk horns for musicians to play. They also shaped ivory and wood into statues, jewelry, boxes, and

Head of a queen mother. Her coral crown and thick coral necklace symbolize her high position and unique powers.

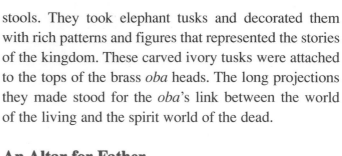

stools. They took elephant tusks and decorated them with rich patterns and figures that represented the stories of the kingdom. These carved ivory tusks were attached to the tops of the brass *oba* heads. The long projections they made stood for the *oba*'s link between the world of the living and the spirit world of the dead.

An Altar for Father

Many of these royal treasures ended up being placed at altars in the palace and in temples. Every *oba* prepared an altar to his father and had artists make objects for it.

Each *oba* also prepared an altar dedicated to his own head, or his destiny. He also had an altar to his hand and arm, the sources of his achievements in life.

These altars were built on a semicircular platform made of hardened mud. Brass scenes of court life stood at the center, surrounded by brass heads and other objects. Rattle staffs—poles with rattles at the ends, to scare away evil spirits—leaned against the wall at the back. These altars were the places to which the *oba* came to make sacrifices and offerings during festivals like Igue.

Country Life

In the towns and villages, chiefs and even ordinary people also constructed altars to their heads and hands and to their ancestors. These altars, of course, were much more simple. Instead of brass and ivory objects, the people placed objects made of wood, coconut shells, and gourds on their altars.

Most things about life in the country were more modest than in the city. Outside Benin City the Edo lived in several hundred villages, most with a population of four or five hundred. The

In addition to brass plaques and religious objects, the oba *filled his palace with everyday objects made of brass. Few others could afford things like this brass incense burner. In modern terms it would be like having solid gold kitchen appliances! To use the burner, a servant would place aromatic spices in the cagelike chamber below the royal rooster. Once ignited, the spices would create fragrant smoke to perfume the* oba*'s rooms.*

rectangular houses faced onto one or two streets and cleared, sandy spaces. The task of farming dominated most days. The farms were not connected to the village, and their location changed every year. Each year villagers cleared new parts of the rain forest and planted one or two plots of yams and other vegetables. They worked three days, and then took a day of rest.

During their leisure hours villagers spent most of their time talking. They had no television, radio, or video games. So they told one another stories about ghosts, about ancient wars and heroes, about the gods. They also played games. The adults played board games. Children played a version of the modern rock-scissors-paper school-yard game. In it, one Edo child held his or her fist out to the other and said, "Ta," which meant "Guess." The other child had to guess how many dice the fist held. If he or she guessed correctly, the first child forfeited the dice. Edo girls played a lot of games that involved songs, the way modern girls do with jump ropes and hand-clapping games. Both boys and girls played rougher games, versions of tug-of-war and red rover.

Even as the villagers and country people went about their lives, they owed absolute obedience to their respective chiefs and to the *oba* in Benin City. As any Edo would say, all the people, whether in the city or the country, were "slaves of the *oba*." The culture of brass and ivory was never far away.

CHAPTER THREE

GODS, SPIRITS, GHOSTS, AND THE *OBA*

In the Edo religion, the gods demanded sacrifices of food and sometimes of animals before they would bestow any favors. Food offerings might be carried to the altar in a basket like the one held by this brass figurine.

In Benin religion took a lot more effort than setting aside one day a week for worship. Spiritual life was complicated. It not only involved a supreme god and a world of the dead, but also a crowd of other, lesser gods. As the Edo prayed and sacrificed and performed rituals honoring their many gods, they had several goals: First, they wanted to live prosperously and die leaving many children and grandchildren. Second, they wanted the kingdom and the *oba* to be rich and powerful. Third, they wanted the gods to grant them favors. Overall, their religion praised life and the community. They prayed for things that would benefit family, village, and kingdom rather than for things that would benefit them personally.

How It All Began

Like almost every other religion, Edo faith began with a story about how the world and the Benin kingdom came to be. This is the story:

Long, long ago, the universe was just one big expanse of water, like an ocean with no end. Only a single tree, as lonely as a clam in its shell, broke the surface of the water. On top of the tree lived a long-beaked bird called Owonwon (OH-wahn-wahn).

One day the supreme god, named Osanobua (oh-san-oh-BOO-ah), decided to create the world. So he sent his three children down to the water: his daughter Obieve (oh-bee-AY-vay) and his two sons, Olokun (OH-low-koon) and Ogiuwu (oh-gee-OOH-woo). As they were about to depart, the Owonwon bird in the lonely tree called out that the three should carry a snail shell with them. So they found a shell, and then paddled to the middle of the watery waste. Then Obieve, the oldest, turned the snail shell upside down, and out poured an endless stream of sand. The sand spread as far as the eye could see, and it became the land.

Osanobua, the supreme god, divided the earth between his three children. He gave Obieve control over childbirth and agriculture. Olokun became the god of the sea. Ogiuwu became the lord of death.

The Edo believed that the world Osanobua had created was divided into two distinct parts: the visible, physical world and the spirit world. Normally, people couldn't see the spirit world, which was the home of the supreme god, lesser gods, souls of the dead and living, and demons and other supernatural beings. This invisible world was directly linked to the visible world. It could affect what happened in the physical world, and did. A lot of Edo worship was aimed at getting the spirits to do nice things instead of bad things. The gods the Edo worshiped may be divided into four types: "personal" gods, ancestor gods, the *oba*, and gods above the *oba*.

Animals, like the crocodile and fish depicted in this brass plaque, held a central place in the beliefs of the Edo people. The crocodile was usually a symbol of strength; the fish of wealth. Since the crocodile, "strength," is eating the fish, "wealth," it might be that the artist meant to show that strength brings riches.

Personal Gods

The *Ehi*: A Spiritual Double

"Personal" gods were those connected to an Edo's person, or body. The center of every Edo's spiritual life was the *ehi* (AY-he). Each living person had an *ehi*. In one sense it was his or her destiny. In

another sense it was a person's "other half," a spiritual double and guide. Each time a person was reborn, he had the same *ehi*. The Edo believed that a person and his *ehi* were joined in one life after another. Some said that a person and his *ehi* took turns being born on earth. In one life, the person was reborn; in the next, the *ehi* was.

Before being born on earth, each person went to *hi* (he) before the supreme god Osanobua. "To *hi*" meant to make a statement before Osanobua. The soon-to-be-born knelt down and explained what he wanted to do in his coming life: whether he wanted to be

LISTEN TO YOUR EHI

Long ago, there was a man named Use (oo-SAY) who lived in wretched poverty. He had no food and no clothes. Year after year he planted crops. But at harvesttime, poor Use had not an ear of corn or a single yam to collect.

One year he decided that he would pray to the supreme god Osanobua every time he went to his field. That year his crops grew abundantly. The corn was thick; the vegetables healthy and large. When harvesttime came, Use went to his field in high spirits. When he reached the field, he was dismayed. In the night wild pigs had broken into his field and eaten up everything. Use broke down and cried. Then he decided to follow the trail of the pigs. The trail led him to a river. Use, desperate, jumped into the river.

He sank underwater, and suddenly found himself in the undersea palace of Osanobua. Use told the supreme god his tale of woe. Osanobua felt sorry for the poor man, so he told him to stay in a dark room. Then Osanobua summoned Use's *ehi*, his spirit double. (Use had to stay in the dark because no living person could see his *ehi* and survive.)

"Use was just here," Osanobua told the *ehi*. "He was telling me how wretched he is."

"Let him suffer!" the *ehi* said. "He did not say he would be a farmer when he went to the world. He said he would grow prosperous as a trapper. But when he got to the world, he forgot his plan and did something else."

Then the *ehi* went home, and Osanobua let Use out of his hiding place.

"Did you hear what the *ehi* said?" Osanobua asked.

"Yes," Use replied.

When Use got back to the world, he immediately set some animal traps. But as he was doing so, he hit something hard in the ground. He dug it up and found it was a pot of beads. They were the most precious kind of bead: Two beads alone would buy a man. So Use returned to town and sold all the beads. He became one of the richest of men.

From that day to this people have said, "If you do not know what your *ehi* has told you, you cannot prosper."

a farmer or a trader, a warrior or a carver, a thief or a chief. Then he asked the god for all the tools and talents needed to accomplish the plan. When the person finished, Osanobua banged his staff on the ground, setting his seal on these wishes. Then the person was born. The *ehi* stayed behind in the spirit world to act as a guide and a contact with Osanobua.

Success in life depended in part on keeping to the plan laid out before birth. "*Ehi* is the way a person has to go," the people said. If, for example, a woman suffered, or had continued misfortune, the Edo said that she did not "*hi* well," or that she had "bad *ehi*." When bad things happened, people made prayers and offerings to their *ehis,* asking them to intervene. After a stroke of good fortune, people thanked their *ehis*. However, being human, they were more likely to call upon them only in times of trouble.

Use Your Head

A prosperous life demanded more than just a good plan. A person also had to rely on judgment, wisdom, and character. The Edo called this *uhumwu* (oo-WHOM-woo), or "head." The head was the seat of thinking, hearing, seeing, and speaking. A person's head led him or her through life. It was linked with luck or fortune. Depending on whether a person was successful or not, people might say that his head was "good" or that it was "bad." The Edo blessed their heads annually, and when they wanted a particular favor. They first thanked their heads for survival and prosperity, then they made their special request. This is part of the reason the Edo placed statues of heads on their altars.

Men, in particular, stressed worship of the head. The welfare of an entire family depended on a man's head. His wives and children would suffer if his head were "bad." Even further, the welfare of the entire kingdom depended on the *oba*'s head. The Ugie Erha Oba festival honored the *oba*'s head, and included human sacrifices to it.

Lend a Hand

The last of the personal gods was the hand, or the arm. The hand represented the ability to accomplish things in the world. It symbolized vigor, or strength, and success in farming, trading, and any

other activity. Warriors, who lived or died by the strength and skill of their hands, usually had altars to their hands. So did the *oba* and particularly wealthy or successful chiefs who had grasped success through their own efforts.

These shrines included a wooden platform carved with a design of clenched fists, meaning "I have caught it!" On top of the platform stood a statue of a hand with the fist clenched and thumb pointing up. Worshipers brought spears, shields, tools, or symbols of wealth such as padlocked chests and cowrie shells to the shrine. During some ceremonies, chiefs wore large cloth cutouts of hands. These were called hands of wealth. They showed that the chiefs had achieved wealth and power through their own efforts or "hand."

A modestly successful person would not have an altar to his hand. "What has my hand done for me?" a mid-level official might say. Someone who failed might say, dejected, "I have no hand."

Witches, Ghosts, and Magic

After their personal deities had been honored and satisfied, people had to go to great lengths to keep the rest of the invisible world in line. At altars they offered food and kola nuts. They erected special shrines all over their houses. On their door beams and thresholds, they attached charms for extra protection.

The Edo fascination with ghosts and witchcraft was no greater than that in Europe and Asia during the same period. In fifteenth-century Europe, people were constantly fooled by promises of miraculous cures, magic potions, and healing fragments of the "true cross." Witch burning was common. At this time, the Chinese and the Japanese also believed in ghosts and magic.

For the Edo, the spirits of the dead and their family ancestors provided the closest contact with the other world. After a person died and was buried properly, the Edo believed, the deceased made a hazardous trip across the waters that surrounded the earth. On the

This hand clutching a mudfish decorated the top of a "rattle staff," a long noisemaker used in religious ceremonies. The hand symbolizes the oba's *power. The coiled mudfish, an animal that can sting, refers specifically to the* oba's *power to punish and pardon, to cast a curse or to release it.*

other side, the deceased entered the spirit world and tried to be accepted there. Once he or she became part of the spirit world, the deceased could interfere with the affairs of the living. The Edo spent a lot of time trying to please the dead in the hope that they would not play tricks on the living.

A modern altar to the hand. The spike may have supported an ivory tusk. Most of the symbols refer to the accumulation of wealth and power.

The problem was that not every person who died was lucky enough to have children to bury him or her properly. If a man or woman died childless, he or she would be stuck in the world as a ghost. These were the phantoms people saw if they were foolish enough to go to their farms on a rest day. Understandably the ghosts were angry at the living; life had not been fair to them. So they tried to hurt the living whenever possible. They also tried to keep the spirits of the properly buried from making it safely to the spirit world. For this reason the Edo threw scraps of food to the ghosts whenever they made sacrifices to their ancestors.

Ghosts weren't the only dangers. Witches and sorcerers knew

how to separate their "life force" from their bodies. In this way they turned themselves into owls, cats, and dogs. They could also transform their victims into prey animals, like goats or antelope, and then slaughter them. Each village had a tree where witches were believed to meet at night and plan their murders. Eziza (ay-ZEE-zah), the bearded and hairy god of the whirlwind, kidnapped those who wandered too far into the forest. Ugly monsters called elders of the night snatched people and carried them off.

To protect themselves from these supernatural threats and other problems, the Edo turned to "witch doctors" and "curing doctors." Witch doctors could fight witchcraft. They went to road junctions, believed to be places where the physical world and the invisible world intersected. There the witch doctors prepared medicines and made sacrifices intended to persuade the witches to stop their evil doings. Witch doctors also claimed to be able to identify witches. They would force suspected witches to undergo tests—snatching cowries out of boiling palm oil, for instance, or forcing feathers through their tongues. Curing doctors tried to help the Edo with personal, rather than supernatural, problems. They were experts at preparing herbal potions to cure the sick. They also developed spiritual powers over many years. Sometimes they went into trances to carry messages to the spirit world. Other times they used fortune-telling methods to try to answer questions, such as why a woman couldn't have children or whether a business would be a success.

The King as Demigod

When it came to personal gods, ghosts, witches, and spirits, every Edo had a slightly different religion. Whether a person sacrificed to his head or his hand, whether he prepared charms against ghosts, whether he suspected someone was using witchcraft against him— all these things depended on individual circumstances. If times were tough, a person might sacrifice to his *ehi* and call in the witch doctor. If times were good, he would thank his head and his hand and have little use for doctors at all. But all Edo absolutely believed in this truth: The *oba* was semidivine, the closest thing to a god that they would ever see.

Edo shrines varied quite a lot. Some might focus on a god, a person's head or hand, or the oba. *Others might be set up temporarily for a specific purpose: to heal someone or to cast a curse. In this modern shrine, a divination plate has been placed in front of two clay figures, which represent deities. The plate holds a few cowrie shells. When shaken, the plate will divine, or predict, future events based on the way the cowries fall.*

The *oba* was powerful and wise, fierce and noble. Some versions of the creation story even said that the *oba* was one of the three gods who helped create the earth. In these renderings of the tale, the *oba*—not Obieve, the goddess of birth—was the one who upended the snail shell and poured out the sand that made the land. The Edo said that because he had created it, the *oba* owned all the land in the world. Other kings were forced to come to the *oba* and ask him for space in which to build their kingdoms.

The *oba* straddled the invisible world between the living and

In this brass plaque a mudfish-legged oba *is supported by two courtiers. However, this plaque is probably not a portrait of Ohen, the* oba *who claimed he had been turned into a mudfish. The scene more likely refers to the belief that the first* oba *rose from the sea and was closely related to Olokun, the sea god.*

the gods. Through him, the gods channeled the powers that protected the Edo people. It was dangerous to look the *oba* in the face because the *oba* had all sorts of magical powers. Unlike mortal men, the Edo believed, the *oba* did not need to eat, sleep, or wash. The servants who waited on him in the palace could not talk about the *oba*'s physical life. The penalty was death for saying, or even hinting, that the *oba* ate and slept. The *oba* could not show any sign of human weakness.

The Edo told many stories about the *obas*. But one in particular makes clear how seriously the Edo took the *oba*'s power. In the fourteenth century an *oba* named Ohen was given the coral crown. Ohen had ruled the kingdom for about twenty-five years when he got sick and could no longer walk. So he told his chiefs that he had been partly transformed into a mudfish, a sacred symbol of royal power. To hide the truth of his disability, Oba Ohen made sure that he was carried into the council chamber before anyone else. He also waited until all his chiefs had left before he had himself carried out again. One day one of the chiefs hid himself and discovered the *oba*'s secret. Furious, Ohen had the chief killed immediately. Gradually, though, the word got out that Oba Ohen was not a mudfish, but a cripple. When the people learned the truth, they stoned Ohen to death.

The moral of this story: The *oba* and the kingdom were one and the same. If the *oba* was weak, then the country might become weak as well. Ohen had revealed all too clearly that he was human. Therefore he could no longer be the *oba*.

Gods above the *Oba*

Even if the *oba* was a god, he certainly was not the most powerful god. That honor fell to Osanobua, the creator of everything in the universe. The Edo pictured him as a king living in splendor with many wives and children. Legend has it that Oba Ewuare sent some of his close followers to visit Osanobua himself. In return Osanobua visited Benin three times. The places where he appeared in the kingdom became the sites of the three major shrines to him.

In general, though, Osanobua did not have a complex system

The people of Benin believed that chalk was a sacred symbol of life and of Osanobua, the supreme god. As this chalk drawing shows, a temporary shrine could be made by simply sketching symbols in chalk on the ground.

of priests and temples to serve him. People believed Osanobua, or Osa, was everywhere. They prayed to him for general things: prosperity, good luck, victory. To ask for Osa's help, an Edo only had to look toward the sun, or insert a branch into the sand and surround it with a few lumps of chalk and cowrie shells to form an altar. If they had requests for Osa, people had to make sacrifices at the altars. Osa only accepted sacrifices of animals. He particularly liked doves.

The Edo actually worshiped Olokun, the god of the sea, with more fervor than they honored Osa. Perhaps this was because they believed that Olokun was the *oba*'s counterpart in the spirit world. The *oba* owned the land. Olokun's name meant "owner of the ocean." The Edo believed that the land of the living was surrounded by limitless water. This was Olokun's realm. All the rivers of the world—Olokun's wives—flowed into it.

The Edo built a large temple to Olokun at Urhonigbe (oor-ru-NEEG-bay). There, priests and priestesses served him. Each year the entire town put on a festival in his honor. Across the kingdom every Edo household had an altar to the god. Worshipers rubbed

THE SACRIFICIAL LAMB, MUDFISH, COW, KOLA NUT . . .

Sacrifices are an important part of many religions. The ancient Hebrews killed lambs to honor their god. The ancient Aztecs of Mexico cut the hearts out of living people to please their many deities. Tribes in Southeast Asia slit the throats of pigs to honor the earth.

Though these practices may seem barbaric today, they were not just random violence. Sacrifices had a deadly serious purpose. It may help to think of them as a cosmic combination of a thank-you note and Christmas wish list. By sacrificing animals, plants, even humans, the devout thanked the gods for the richness of the earth and for its rebirth each spring. Then, after they had given something back to the gods, believers asked them to keep creating wealth and renewing the land each year.

Sacrifices were a major part of Benin's religion. People left their offerings at altars to the *oba,* to their ancestors, to local gods, and to national gods. Palm wine, mudfish, and kola nuts were the most common offerings on ordinary days. The Edo saved blood sacrifices—roosters, goats, sheep, dogs, and cows—for special occasions. Afterward, those who had participated in the ritual divided the meat and cooked it. Only the *oba* could order a human sacrifice; the corpse was not eaten. At all times, the business of sacrificing was governed by a dizzying number of rules. Here are some of them:

• Some deities—Osanobua, the supreme god; Olokun, the sea god; and Obieve, the goddess of birth—were associated with the color white. Thus, sacrifices to them were also supposed to be white: doves, cowrie shells, coconut, white cotton. Olokun, the sea god, accepted goats and white birds.

• Other gods—Ogun, the god of iron and war, and Osun, the medicine god—were associated with the color red. Sacrifices to them were supposed to be red: young red roosters, red dogs. These gods also loved traditional "fast foods": roasted red yam and red palm oil. Ogun liked turtles and snails as well.

• Ogiuwu, the god of death, demanded big sacrifices: humans, cows, goats, and rams. These offerings to Ogiuwu could not be eaten. Instead they had to be allowed to rot away.

• Ghosts, especially evil ones, could be appeased with an offering of their favorite treat, called *izobo* (ee-ZOH-bow), or "ambrosia of the gods": portions of sacrificial liver, kidney, and intestines.

In honor of Ogun, the god of war, these acrobats perform an ancient dance that recalls a legendary war against the sky. Above perch ibises, birds of disaster.

themselves with white chalk, a symbol of purity. They prayed to Olokun for children and for wealth.

Ogun (oh-GOON), or Ogu, the god of iron, also command-ed a large following. Legend said that Ogun used his machete, a large curved knife, to clear a pathway through the jungle when the gods first came to earth. Because of his skill with the machete, Ogun became the god of hunters, blacksmiths, butchers, barbers, and soldiers. In forges, where blacksmiths made tools and horse-shoes, altars to Ogun always occupied a central place. Hunters and warriors made sacrifices at their altars to Ogun before they went on their expeditions. When they returned they placed the skulls of their victims in front of their Ogun shrines. The Edo said that a curse in Ogun's name was particularly effective: Ogun killed violently.

In contrast people turned to Osu (oh-SUE), the god of medicine, for more gentle help. The people would make a shrine to Osu at a large tree deep in the forest. There, worshipers left big pots full of rainwater and leaves, the stuff of medicine. Bathing in the water from these pots strengthened a person for a difficult task or a long journey. It also protected against enemies in war. In most Edo households, the head of the fam-ily had a shrine to Osu in a special room where he kept his medicines.

Obieve, the eldest daughter of Osanobua, originally oversaw childbirth, but her role in that area was gradually taken over by Olokun. No one, however, dared to challenge Ogiuwu, the god of death. When it was time to die, Ogiuwu came for people, sort of like the Grim Reaper. No images of Ogiuwu existed. No artist dared to draw the face of death. People worshiped Ogiuwu at a central shrine in Benin City, where they sacrificed human slaves before the army marched into battle. Chiefs and others sacrificed cows to the god, hoping to get him to delay calling for them. Edo everywhere feared Ogiuwu. They called him "the merciless son of God who eats the kola nut and doesn't spare the shell."

Ofoe, messenger of Ogiuwu, the "merciless" god of death.

CHAPTER FOUR

WHICH CAME FIRST, BENIN OR ITS CULTURE?

Do people live a certain way because of what they believe? Or do people believe certain things because of how and where they live?

In Benin a person could answer yes to both questions. Edo ideas about religion and about the *oba* affected a decision to go to war, how to pay taxes, how to spend most days. At the same time, the people of Benin were deeply influenced by their experiences. Their environment often affected what they believed. Real people who did great things gradually became gods who were worshiped at altars and shrines. Places where important things happened became sacred, so shrines were built there. And established gods might become more or less popular depending on what was going on in the kingdom.

A brass hip ornament like this one could only be worn by chiefs and those to whom the oba *had granted court titles such as Tax Collector or Keeper of the Royal Regalia.*

A Rank for Everyone

Nothing affected day-to-day life more than the absolute power of the *oba*. He, the god-king, was the center of the nation. The Edo called him "Child of the Sky whom we pray not to fall and cover us up; child of the Earth whom we beg not to swallow us up."

Since the *oba* was so powerful, his favor was necessary to do anything important. To get to the *oba,* you had to gain the favor of the *oba*'s senior chiefs. To get to the senior chiefs, you had to win the notice of the junior chiefs. To get to the junior chiefs, you had to make friends with the junior chiefs' servants and messengers. You see the idea.

With the *oba* at the top, everyone in Benin had a rank. To do certain things, you had to have the correct rank. Some ranks led.

In Benin, rank was everything, as this brass plaque shows. The warrior chief in the center is the most important figure. The two warriors at each side are slightly smaller. The attendants are the smallest of all, reflecting their low status.

Some followed. This is called a hierarchy (HI-uh-rar-kee). Top to bottom, Edo chiefs, men, wives, children, and even slaves were arranged into an enormous system of ranks.

It was as if the entire kingdom were divided into grades, just like there are grades in school. But the Edo system was much more complicated. If your school were organized like old Benin, it wouldn't just have grades one, two, three, and so on. It would have grades, and then grades within grades. So in the sixth grade there

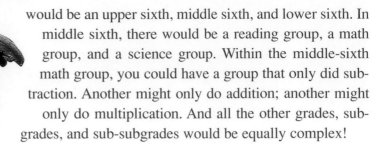

would be an upper sixth, middle sixth, and lower sixth. In middle sixth, there would be a reading group, a math group, and a science group. Within the middle-sixth math group, you could have a group that only did subtraction. Another might only do addition; another might only do multiplication. And all the other grades, subgrades, and sub-subgrades would be equally complex!

The Big Three

Hundreds of ranks and grades divided Edo society, but three groups of chiefs stood out from the rest: the *uzama* (ooh-ZAH-mah), the palace chiefs, and the town chiefs.

Of these the *uzama* commanded the most respect. Long, long ago, the *uzama*'s ancestors sent the messenger to Ife, asking the *oni* of Ife to send a ruler to Benin. So each time a new *oba* of Benin took the throne, he went through a ceremony in which he "bought" the land of the kingdom from the original owners, the *uzama*. Some people said that the *uzama* "owned" the *oba*. Many of the *uzama*'s duties involved ceremony and ritual. They also made up the state council that helped the *oba* make decisions. With all this to do in Benin City, the *uzama* did not have time to leave their palaces and work to create great wealth. For power they had to rely on their reputations. They passed their titles from father to son. Because they were almost like kings, the *uzama* often got into arguments with the *oba*.

The palace chiefs, in contrast, controlled direct access to the *oba*. By insisting that people pay for their help in getting the *oba*'s attention, the palace chiefs could get very rich. They ran the three "palace associations," or *otu* (OH-too): the *iwebo* (ee-WEH-bow), which cared for the king's robes and ritual duties; the *iweguae* (ee-WEG-gwah), which saw to the *oba*'s personal needs; and the *ibiwe* (ee-BEE-way), which supervised the *oba*'s wives and children. Even though these chiefs could not pass their titles directly to their sons, they could give them the money and advice necessary to succeed. So in practice, the palace chiefs worked like nobles who passed their money and status down from generation to generation.

Unlike either the *uzama* or the palace chiefs, the town chiefs

Brass roosters were placed on altars to the queen mothers of Benin and were a symbol of their high status. A rooster is a male creature, one that literally crows over its maleness. It symbolizes the fact that the queen mother, unlike other women, shares many privileges with the powerful men at court.

A junior court official. His few ornaments indicate that he has yet to rise through the ranks of a palace association.

rose to power through their own efforts. By farming, trading, or succeeding in some other way, they came to the notice of the *oba,* who then gave them titles. They took care of the lands and territories outside Benin City. They collected taxes and made sure that roads were built and that public buildings such as shrines were kept up. They had more contact with the common people than the other leaders. Some called them the voice of the people.

The geography of Benin City reflected the relationships between the *oba* and his chiefs. The *oba*'s palace and the homes of the palace chiefs took up the southwest quarter of the capital. The town chiefs lived outside the palace walls, in the northwest part of the city. The *uzama* had palaces of their own.

Did the Average Person Care about All This?

The politics of the capital and the palace raged far above the life of the average Edo. Yet the influence of Benin City could reach down to the most humble village street or country courtyard. The entire kingdom of Benin was divided into sections, like counties in the United States. The *oba* put a chief in charge of each section: a cluster of villages here, a district surrounding a large town there. The town chiefs tended to have more of these sections, but the palace chiefs and *uzama* also had responsibility for some of them. One chief might have several sections, scattered all over the kingdom.

Country people had to be mindful of this system. Twice a year each section had to send tribute, or taxes, to the capital: yams, cloth, vegetables, livestock, even slaves. Their chief would take part of this tribute for himself. The rest would go to the *oba* and the royal palace. Villages also had to provide laborers for jobs such as building new palaces or repairing roads. If the villages didn't contribute, they were considered rebels, and the *oba*'s army would attack them. So villagers ignored the capital at their peril.

The Rank and File

The common people also had their own system of ranks and grades, which mirrored those of the *oba* and his chiefs. At the palace court, in the villages, even within families, the Edo saw relationships between people in terms of master and servant. That is, people were never equals. One person was always the superior and the other person was always the junior.

In the villages men were divided into three grades, according to their age. At about age sixteen, boys joined the most junior group: the *iroghae* (ee-ROW-guy). They became responsible for the hard physical work that the community needed. From about age thirty until fifty, men were *ighele* (EE-gay-lay). They supervised the younger men and defended the village. After fifty, men became *edion* (ay-dee-OHN), or elders. They no longer had to do hard physical work, and spent most of their time resolving disputes among the people.

Women were not formally organized like the men. But people did group them according to which women were married, which had children, and which did not.

Even within the family, people had very definite ranks. Those who were men, and who were older, always had more power. For instance the head of a family considered his wives and his children to be his servants. The Edo word for *wife* could also mean "my boy" or "my servant." When men greeted one another on the street, they said, "Are your people well?" The greeting implied that a man, in a sense, owned his family. He had the power to tell his family what to do, what to eat, what to wear. He could even punish them physically—beat them—if he thought it necessary.

The Edo genius for organizing everything extended not only to chiefs, villages,

A brass sculpture of a girl holding a small leopard. The leopard—symbol of the oba—*may indicate that she is of royal blood.*

and families, but also to professions. All the craftsmen of the kingdom belonged to guilds, or unions, similar to those in medieval Europe. Membership in the guilds, and secrets of the crafts, passed from father to son. These groups included brass casters, ivory carvers, wood carvers, bead and costume makers, and leather workers. In all, more than sixty-eight crafts were organized this way. Often, members of the same guild lived in the same neighborhood and had their workshops on the same street.

Making Hierarchy Work

One absolute—that the *oba* was the ultimate leader—spawned the enormous, complicated hierarchy that was the Benin kingdom. However, living in Benin was not as neat and tidy as all the ranks and grades might sound. Everyone, even the *oba,* tried to influence the system so that it worked best for them. To maintain his power, the *oba* had to make sure that none of the chiefs had too much control over any one thing. He tried to keep chiefs competing with each other by granting titles to one and not to another. He gave chiefs sections of the country to administer, but made sure that none of them were close together. The chiefs, for their part, were all trying to flatter the *oba* and trick him into giving them more titles and power. The people all tried to bribe the chiefs to give favors to them. You could say that Benin was like a giant board game: All the Edo were trying to get a monopoly, while the *oba* was trying to prevent that so that he could control the Monopoly board himself!

On Becoming a God

The belief that the *oba* was a demigod—and the hierarchy that idea created—affected every Edo, from highest to lowest. But sometimes it could work the other way: People and places could become godlike. Most villages had several "cults," or groups of believers dedicated to a god that did not have a national following. The deity might be a part of the landscape, like a mountaintop or a valley. Or it might be a famous person from the past.

For instance every brass caster in Benin had an altar to

IF YOU LIVED IN ANCIENT BENIN

If you had been born during Benin's greatest time, the fifteenth and sixteenth centuries, your way of life would have been determined by the facts of your birth—whether you were a boy or a girl, free or slave, wealthy or poor. With this chart you can trace the course your life might have taken as a citizen of Benin.

You were born in Benin City. . . .

As a Boy . . .   **As a Girl . . .**

You live in a house made of dried mud brick and roofed with tightly bound branches and grasses. The house has ten to twenty rooms facing a central courtyard. Seven days after your birth—when the family thinks you are likely to survive—you receive a name.

At age 7 you accompany your father when he goes to work on the yam farm. Your father teaches you his skills: If he's a farmer, you learn to plant and clear land. If he's a craftsman, you learn his skills. If he's a chief, you start to learn about politics.

▼

At about age 16 you join the lowest rank for men. You become responsible for the "heavy lifting" in the community: clearing roads and paths, carrying mud for house building. You start a yam farm of your own, get married, and bring your first wife home to live in your father's house. After you earn enough to have a second wife, you build a house of your own.

▼

At about age 30 you join the second rank for adult males. Now your main goals are having as many sons as you can, marrying many wives, and buying slaves who can farm for you and make you rich. You work hard to get appointed to a government position.

▼

At about age 50 you are a senior government official and an elder in the community. You often tell stories, handing down Edo traditions and customs.

At age 7 you go with your mother to her small vegetable garden. You learn how to go to market and sell the vegetables that your mother grows. Very quickly, you master the skill of balancing small loads on your head. Sometime during your childhood, you become engaged. Your family has arranged a marriage for you with the son of a local family.

▼

At about age 16 you get married in a big ceremony. Your husband's family comes for you and you go to live with them. As a young bride you have to do whatever your husband's mother tells you to do. Once you have had a son, your position in the family is secure.

▼

As you get older you focus on raising your children and keeping your husband happy. The vegetable crops are yours to sell at the market. The money you earn is yours to spend as you wish.

You do not assume an official title as an elder, but you informally perform for women many duties: settling arguments, overseeing rituals, maintaining traditions.

You die after having had many children. Your funeral is a cause to celebrate as well as to grieve, and your children erect or rededicate an altar to your memory.

Igeugha (ee-GOO-eye) in his workshop. Iguegha was born in Yorubaland, about a hundred miles from Benin. In the late thirteenth century, the *oba* of Benin sent to the *oni* of Ife for someone to teach his subjects how to cast brass. The *oni* sent Igeugha and some of his assistants. Igeugha taught the Edo people to use the lost-wax method of brass casting. He showed them how to make statues out of brass and how to decorate them. He became respected throughout the kingdom. After Iguegha died, his students began to make sacrifices to his memory. Gradually, the master brass caster became a god.

The Faithful Wife

Sometimes a person might become a god by doing something really unusual. Ovia (OH-vee-ah) did. Edo legend said that Ovia was a beautiful girl who lived a long time ago. Many men wanted to marry her. But Ovia said that she would marry only a king. When she grew up, the news of her beauty reached the *oba*. He sent word to her father, asking for Ovia's hand in marriage. Ovia's father obeyed, but he feared that his daughter's marriage might end badly. So he gave Ovia a magical pot, a dog, and a parrot. He told his daughter that if her husband ever treated her badly, she could pass through the pot and come home.

With the gifts from her father, Ovia set off for Benin City. She caught the eye of the *oba* as soon as she arrived. He loved her fine clothes and her beauty. Ovia soon became the *oba*'s favorite wife. This made Ovia and the *oba* happy, but it made all the *oba*'s other wives angry and jealous. One of the senior wives tricked the *oba* into believing that Ovia was sick. She told the *oba* that if he continued to spend so much time with Ovia, he would get sick, too. At first the *oba* believed the senior wife and stayed away from Ovia. Then all the wives laughed at Ovia and made her miserable.

After a while, though, the *oba* began to doubt the warnings of the senior wife. He decided to go see Ovia. When he got to Ovia's room, he saw that she had been crying for a long time. As the *oba*

This ivory spoon was no doubt made by a member of the ivory-carving guild that lived in a special district of Benin City. If the spoon was meant for use by the oba, *it was probably made by a senior member of the carvers' guild. In Benin even crafts were segregated by rank.*

watched, Ovia melted away into a shower of tears. The tears fell into the pot that Ovia's father had given her. They became a river that flowed out of the palace and back to Ovia's father. When Ovia got home she told her father that no woman should ever know her secrets because it was women who forced her to leave her husband's house.

From that time forward, men in many villages formed groups to worship Ovia as a goddess. To remember the dog she took to the palace, they sacrificed dogs to her memory. To remember the parrot she took to the palace, they wore parrot feathers in their hair. Every so often they would retreat to Ovia's shrines in the forest. For several days they would speak a secret language. They danced and, in various ceremonies, asked Ovia to bless their friends and family and to curse their enemies. No women were permitted to take part in these rituals. In the end, Ovia got her revenge on other women!

Spirit of Place

Places could also become sacred or haunted if something special happened there. Aruanran (ah-roo-AHN), the giant half-brother of Oba Esigie (eh-SEEG-ee-ay), tried to become *oba* by fighting his brother at the village of Udo. Aruanran failed, but the people of Udo came to believe that he turned into a nearby lake. Legend says that his spirit comes out of the lake every so often. The spirit leaves telltale footprints in both directions.

Before Ewuare became the *oba* in the fifteenth century, he was sent away from Benin and forbidden to return. But Ewuare visited the capital secretly anyway. The chiefs found out, and Ewuare had to run for his life. First, he hid in a dried-up well. Then he ran into the forest with his sword and his spear. During the night, Ewuare rested under a tree.

Just as he was falling asleep, he felt something like water drop on his head. In the morning, he realized that blood had been dripping on his head. He looked up, and saw a leopard with blood dribbling from its mouth. He jumped up in surprise and realized that he had been lying on a snake all night. He killed the leopard and the snake and planted a tree nearby. He swore that if he ever became *oba,* he would make the place where he had safely slept that night a place for worshiping his destiny.

After he became *oba,* Ewuare kept his promise. He first commanded people to watch and protect the tree he had planted the night he hid in the forest. Then, once a year, Oba Ewuare sacrificed a leopard at that spot to give thanks because he had become *oba.* After he died, the *obas* who followed him continued the tradition.

Influences on Culture

The situation and experience of the Edo people not only influenced what and where they worshiped, it influenced their culture as well. This was especially true of their art. During the reigns of the early *obas,* Edo brass artists used certain generally recognized royal subjects for all their work: *obas,* chiefs, leopards, elephants, birds of prophecy, and other symbols of power and kingship. Then, in the fifteenth century, Portuguese traders arrived on the coast of West Africa. They brought riches and brass. Some of them even served in the army of the *oba.* A new royal subject was added to the brass artist's repertoire: the Portuguese.

Many brass statues and plaques of the Portuguese were made in the 1500s and 1600s. The Europeans can be picked out by their long hair, beaklike noses, and heavy clothes. Edo statues showed the Portuguese riding horses, as well as aiming guns and crossbows. They also depicted *manillas,* the rings of brass that the sailors traded for slaves, pepper, and ivory.

Some scholars have suggested that the arrival of the Europeans and wealth from across the sea also increased the importance of the Edo god of the sea, Olokun. The seagoing Portuguese added to the kingdom's riches, and they dealt exclusively with the king. They fit perfectly into Edo ideas that linked the *oba* with the sea and with the prosperity of the kingdom. After the fifteenth century, the sea god Olokun became more important to the Edo than his father, Osanobua, the creator of the world. The Edo built many shrines and temples to Olokun, but Osanobua had to be satisfied mostly with household altars built in his honor.

A Benin artist sculpted this brass image of a Portuguese soldier.

CHAPTER FIVE

HOW BENIN LIVES ON TODAY

Even today, the oba *celebrates ancient ceremonies each year.*

enin enjoys an unusual distinction among the great civilizations of the past: It survives almost intact. An ancient Egyptian or Chinese person would be completely bewildered by modern Egypt or China. But if an Edo from the fifteenth century suddenly time-traveled to the present, he would find his modern descendants familiar. Their politics, art, and religion would not be terribly different from his own. "Ancient Benin" really only ended with the British invasion one hundred years ago. And Benin has changed, certainly, but it has not changed so much that it is unrecognizable. Not only that, but because of the slave trade, bits of Edo religion and culture have traveled to many different parts of North and South America and have survived to this day. Benin's music has influenced modern jazz and rock. Its art has become famous the world over. Because the African kola nut is a major ingredient in the drink we call cola, even the corporate giants Coca-Cola and PepsiCo owe a debt to Benin and its West African neighbors!

A Kingdom within a Nation

The descendants of the *oba* and his chiefs do not live in the modern West African nation called the Republic of Benin, though that nation was named in honor of the Benin empire. Old Benin is located to the east, in what is now modern Nigeria. Benin City is located in

Acrobats form a human pillar outside the royal palace in Benin City. Entertainers like these performed for the oba *centuries ago.*

The kola nut looks like an unlikely candidate for world popularity. Small, reddish brown kola nuts are actually seeds that come from the pod of a tree native to Africa. When chewed, these seeds have a bitter taste, but their effect is surprisingly powerful—like taking caffeine, nicotine, and aspirin together. Africans say the kola nut can make a tired man carry an eighty-pound load on his head, help a sick person keep down food, and even increase the courage of a nervous bridegroom!

Kola nuts have long been a part of life in Benin. In old Benin people offered kola nuts as a sacrifice to the gods. The *oba* gave his chiefs kola nuts during certain ceremonies. Ordinary people presented kola nuts to visiting guests as a sign of politeness. Today people sell kola nuts on the streets of Nigerian cities, Benin City included.

You've probably had a little bit of kola nut yourself. It's one of the main ingredients in Coca-Cola, Pepsi, and other cola soft drinks.

Jacob's Pharmacy in Atlanta was the first to sell Coca-Cola in 1886. The ingredients included fruit syrup, dried leaves from the South American coca plant, and an extract of kola nut. The pharmacy advertised it as a cure for headaches and hangovers. It enjoyed modest success. But Coca-Cola didn't become popular until carbonated water was added to it. Then it was sold at the soda fountain as a soft drink rather than as a medicine. Suddenly people couldn't drink it fast enough.

Since then cola has become a phenomenon. It is the most popular drink in the world. People have composed songs about it, written about it, even fought over it. "Rum and Coca-Cola" was a popular tune during World War II. The famous playwright Arthur Miller once joked, "Life without Coca-Cola is unthinkable." During the 1980s there was even a "cola war" as the Coca-Cola and PepsiCo companies fought to dominate the market for the soft drink. The rest of the world now has discovered what the Edo have known for centuries: Cola (kola) is the real thing.

Nigeria's Edo state. From the late nineteenth century until 1960, Nigeria was a colony of Great Britain. Today Nigeria is an independent nation. But within that nation, there still lives a king. His name is Oba Erediauwa (air-DEE-ow-wah).

An *Oba* in a Modern Age

The *oba* no longer leads armies. Nor does he hold the power of life and death over his subjects. Those powers belong to the national Nigerian government. Yet the political power of the *oba* remains unrivaled among those who speak the Edo language. In the decades since independence, Nigeria as a whole has suffered political turmoil. A series of politicians and generals have led the country, and they have not always done it well. Through all the ups and downs at the national level, the *oba* of Benin has reigned unchallenged.

Benin City has become a metropolis with modern office towers and streets clogged with traffic. The discovery of oil in the Niger Delta has made Benin City prosperous, much as trade in spices and slaves once did. Yet amid all this bustle, the *oba*'s palace still stands.

In modern times the *oba* has concentrated on preserving the heritage of his people. When Nigerian politics have been unstable, the *oba* has provided meaning and structure for the lives of the Edo-speaking people. During the 1950s, when Nigeria was still a British colony, Edo festivals were confined to a ten-day period around the modern New Year. But since Nigerian independence, the *obas* have gradually revived more and more of the old ceremonies. Of course the Edo no longer sacrifice human beings, but many of the old ways live on in the *oba*'s palace.

A modern, high-ranking chief sits on a porch, probably waiting for a palace ceremony to begin. Large "hand of wealth" cutouts, which show that he has become rich through his own efforts, are still worn today.

An Edo Renaissance

The British took all the royal treasure when they captured Benin City in 1897. Those beautiful brass heads, ivory tusks, and other masterpieces ended up scattered all over the world, in art galleries, museums, and private collections. The spread of Edo art created international respect for the ancient artists of Benin, but it didn't help the Edo people much.

When a new *oba*, Eweka II, took the throne in 1914, he had to begin the process of remaking all the treasure that had been stolen. He needed large numbers of artists who could make coral-bead garments, cast brass sculptures, carve ivory elephant tusks, and weave traditional fabrics. Eweka II founded the Benin Arts and Crafts School. There, teachers trained a new generation of Edo artists. The

The last three obas *have tried to support a rebirth of traditional crafts. This woodcarver in Benin City may be working on a carving for the palace, or one for the tourist trade.*

art of Benin was reborn; it had a renaissance. Today, the guilds of Edo artists again occupy the same streets they did hundreds of years ago. Not only do they make treasures for the *oba* to use in ceremonies, but they also create objects for sale to art collectors and tourists.

ART THAT STUNNED THE WORLD

No one outside West Africa had ever heard of the brass artwork of Benin until the twentieth century. This was because all of these masterpieces were locked up in the *oba*'s palace. Few foreigners entered the *oba*'s palace, and those who did were traders and adventurers, not art historians. Then in 1897, the British captured Benin City and took all the brass artwork they found in the *oba*'s palace. When the pieces arrived in London, they caused a sensation. The natural lines and beauty of the Benin statues impressed everyone in the art world.

The artistry and the technology needed to produce these statues was obviously very great. At first many European experts refused to believe that brass casters in an African kingdom buried in the forest could have developed the technique all by themselves. They said that the Portuguese must have taught the Edo how to do it. Since then, happily, the Edo artists have been cleared of all doubt. Several studies have proven that the technique of brass casting in Africa predated the arrival of the Europeans.

While much of the *oba*'s brass treasure ended up in British museums, many masterpieces of Benin art can now be found in museums all over the world: Berlin, Hamburg, Cologne, Stuttgart, Vienna, Philadelphia, New York City, and Chicago. Private collectors and dealers trade Benin art. In 1958 the wealthy American Nelson A. Rockefeller paid more than fifty thousand dollars, an enormous sum then, for a sixteenth-century ivory mask from Benin. Famous art dealers sell Edo art. Today thousands of works of brass sculpture from Benin can be found, and admired, all over the world.

New Day for Old Gods

Along with the art of the old days, Edo religious beliefs have survived remarkably well. Despite centuries of challenge from Christian missionaries and the effects of modern television and movies, Edo people follow the traditional ways. The shrines and the pageants, the fortune-tellers and witch doctors—all draw many believers, even among the Edo youth. The old ideas still play a vital role in Edo society.

The sea god Olokun commands devotion in modern Benin City. Almost every household includes an altar to Olokun. A home might even have more than one altar to Olokun: one for each woman, and then one for the head of the household. Every four days, the traditional Edo week, people place offerings on the altar and pray to Olokun. White chalk, a common offering to Olokun, still represents purity and happiness. When someone receives good news, the Edo say, "He has a stomach full of chalk."

The women of Benin still revere Olokun as a guardian of childbirth. Here a woman and her daughter sit before an Olokun shrine dedicated to pregnancy and childbirth. The woman will use the bell she is holding to summon the spirit.

In old Benin, Ogun, the god of iron, protected blacksmiths, hunters, and soldiers. In modern Benin, Ogun is the patron of truck drivers, taxi drivers, and ironworkers. Most traditional households have an altar dedicated to Ogun, where they offer pieces of scrap metal to the god. Taxi drivers carry Ogun's symbol, a miniature hammer and forging tongs, for protection. In court, a traditional Edo swears to tell the truth over a piece of iron, Ogun's symbol. Since Ogun kills violently, no one would dare break an oath to him.

People continue to make sacrifices of animals and foods to the gods. Several years ago, a series of deadly road accidents plagued a central street in Benin City. The city leaders banned street vendors from selling roasted yams and red palm oil there. These are Ogun's favorite foods, the leaders reasoned. They blamed the accidents on Ogun's craving for the yam and palm oil that everyone but he was eating!

Modern Witchcraft

In addition to the worship of the *oba* and the major gods, the Edo still have faith in herbal remedies, witchcraft, charms, and fortune-tellers. Stalls in the markets of Benin City sell everything that priests and witch doctors might need: dried heads of eagles and vultures, crocodile skins, bush rats, and monkeys. Jars full of medicinal leaves and bark sit next to mounds of cowrie shells and chunks of white chalk; tools for fortune-telling share space with brass and iron cutouts of vulture beaks to be offered to the gods.

In Nigeria's Edo state, there are perhaps a hundred times more witch doctors and herbal doctors than there are modern medical doctors. Many villagers find western-style hospitals frightening. If they have a life-threatening injury, they may end up in the emergency room of a hospital. But for less serious complaints—minor illness, a problem having children, a business failure, or marital problems—most Edo will consult a traditional healer. Among other things, these old-fashioned priests and doctors heal minor injuries, help people deal with feelings of grief and loss, and resolve minor disputes. They provide social services that are not always available from the modern government.

From time to time, old, old beliefs have become tangled up with modern politics. In 1944 a chief of Benin City went to a priest

*A traditional doctor treats
a patient.*

because he was angry about what certain people said about him. The priest told him to prepare a charm consisting of the heads of a swallow, a squirrel, and a snake, together with a human skull and various other things. After being ground up, the mixture was placed in shrines dedicated to a god called Owegbe. The charm was supposed to stop people from saying bad things about the chief. Gradually, many people came to worship Owegbe, and a cult grew up around the god. About 250 shrines, each with a political committee, were founded. In the late 1950s and early 1960s, the chief used the Owegbe movement to influence voters and politics.

Benin Gods Overseas

When enslaved Africans were forced to travel across the Atlantic to the Americas, they brought their gods with them. Many traditions from Benin and its neighbors in West Africa—the ancient lands of the Yoruba and Dahomey—survive in the Americas. Historians have not yet traced the exact relationships among these states, but their peoples seem to have worshiped many of the same gods. As a result these deities still have followings in places as far-flung as Brazil and Cuba, Miami and New York City.

In Benin they call the sea god Olokun. In Brazil they have turned Olokun into a female and renamed her Iemanja (ay-MAHNjah). In Benin the people believe that all the rivers of the world flow into Olokun. In Brazil many people of African descent believe that the rivers of the world spring forth from Iemanja's breasts. This goddess of the sea has become one of the most important deities in Brazil. Shrines to her fill the inland city of Bahia. In Rio de Janeiro people flock to the beach on New Year's Eve to ask for Iemanja's blessing. Residents of the city of Salvador give a feast for Iemanja on the second day of February. They gather on the seashore, where they sing songs, make wishes, and give one another presents.

Ogun, the Edo god of iron, has become Ogum (oh-GUM), the

In Bahia, Brazil, a priestess of Iemanja—the Brazilian counterpart to the Benin god Olokun—sits in front of her shrine.

A believer in Bahia wears a serpent headdress. In Benin the serpent is associated with wealth and power. In Brazil it is supposed to bring divine energy and creative power to earth.

god of war in Brazil. Just as some Edo will swear an oath over a piece of iron, so some Brazilians prove they are telling the truth this way: They say the name of Ogum and then place a knife blade to their tongues. In Cuba believers honor Ogun with a bucket-shaped iron cauldron full of iron objects: nails, horseshoes, and arrows. When Cubans migrated to Miami, they brought this tradition with them.

Other deities have also found new homes in the Americas. The Edo god of medicine, Osu, has become Osanyin (oh-SOY-yeen), and he is worshiped in Haiti, Rio de Janeiro, Havana, and

New York City. Xango (SAHN-go), the Edo god of thunder, has become Esango (ay-SAHN-go). He is so popular in the Brazilian city of Recife that his name is used to refer to all religious groups of West African origin. In New York City, worshipers at the Harlem Yoruba Temple have honored Esango (spelled *Shango* there) with a plaster statue and shrine.

Benin and Pop Culture

Even those who do not worship African gods—people who have never heard of Ogun, Osu, and Xango—may owe a debt to Edo culture every time they turn on the radio to listen to jazz or rock music. This cannot be directly proven because the Edo did not have a way to write down their music. But it is generally accepted that African rhythms and instruments had a strong influence on modern musicians, everyone from the jazz trumpeter Dizzy Gillespie to the rapper Ice Cube. These musicians developed songs with several rhythms accompanied by drums—a style considered

Many symbolic charms decorate this piece of fabric worn today by priests and priestesses of Olokun. The cowrie shells, for example, represent Olokun's connection to the sea and wealth.

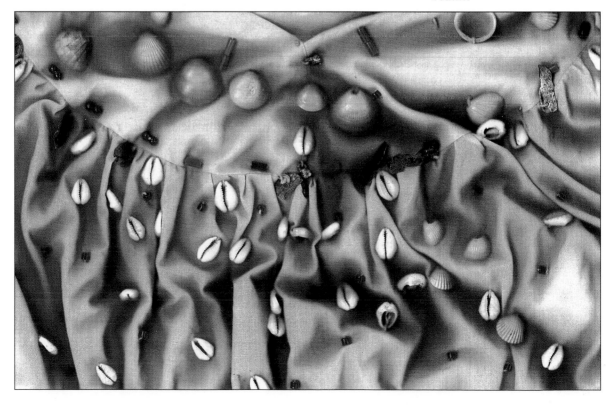

typically African and especially typical of the Niger-Congo River area where Benin is located.

Benin's influence shows in many small ways as well. Cowrie shells, which the Edo used as money well into the twentieth century, are sewn onto modern clothes and used in modern jewelry. Being calm and cool was a goal of most traditional Africans, the Edo as well. This concept comes into play every time someone calls out the modern slang word, *cool!*

Benin's Legacy

An *oba* from the fifteenth century might be disappointed that his country no longer has an army that strikes fear into the hearts of its enemies. He would probably, however, consider it a great achievement that his culture has survived when so many others have not. He would be amazed that Edo sculpture, music, and traditions have reached around the world. All in all, he would be proud of the modern kingdom of Benin.

Modern women in Nigeria perform a dance dedicated to Sango, the god of thunder. The god's favorite color is red.

The Kingdom of Benin: A Chronology

C.E.

c. 900	The ancestors of the Edo immigrate to the Niger Delta
c. 1000	The first of the *ogisos,* or "rulers of the sky," controls Benin
c. 1200	Prince Oranmiyan comes from Ife to Benin
c. 1300	Eweka I becomes the first *oba* of Benin
c. 1440	Ewuare the Great is crowned; under his rule a new palace is built and the empire expands
c. 1481	Oba Ozolua comes to the throne and further enlarges the kingdom
1486	Portuguese traders arrive on the coast near Benin
1516	Christian missionaries from Europe arrive in Benin
1600–1700	Benin society declines in power temporarily
1700	Oba Ewuakpe restores Benin's power
1715	Oba Akenzua I presides over rich trade with Europe
1735	Oba Eresonyen becomes one of the richest *obas* to rule Benin
1800	The power of the *obas* weakens
1896	James Phillips asks to visit Oba Ovonrramwen; Phillips and his party are attacked by the Edo
1897	British troops capture Benin City; Oba Ovonrramwen is banished
1914	Oba Eweka II is crowned by the British
1933	Oba Eweka II dies; his son is crowned Oba Akenzua II
1960	Nigeria becomes independent of Great Britain
1978–1979	Oba Akenzua II dies; his son is crowned Oba Erediauwa

NOTE: Because Benin's history was recorded orally until only recently, dates are approximate until the arrival of the Europeans in the fifteenth century.

Glossary

bird of prophecy: legendary bird with a cry that was supposed to foretell disaster. In the sixteenth century Oba Esigie was marching into battle and heard the bird cry. He ordered the bird killed, and won the battle. When he returned to Benin City, he had artists create clappers in the shape of the bird. These noise-makers have been used in court ritual ever since.

cowrie shell: small oval seashell that was used as money in Benin and in many other African countries

eben (eh-BEN) **sword:** ceremonial sword with a blade shaped like a fan

Edo (EE-doe)**:** the name of the Benin people and their language; also the name of the Nigerian state in which Benin City is located today

ehi (AY-he)**:** Edo person's "other half" in the spirit world; a spiritual guide

hands of wealth: decorated cloth cutouts shaped like large hands; worn by chiefs at ceremonies to symbolize the wealth that their efforts, or "hand," had created

Igue (EE-goo-ay)**:** palace festival to revitalize the king's spiritual powers and thereby strengthen all of Benin

kola nut: seeds from the pod of a West African tree. Small, reddish brown, these nuts were chewed for their stimulant effect and were also a common offering to the gods.

lost-wax casting: process used to make the famous Benin brass statues. The statue was first modeled out of wax, and then covered with clay. The clay was then heated to make all the wax drain out. Then molten metal was poured into the mold. Finally, when the metal was cooled and hardened, the clay mold was broken and stripped away to reveal the statue.

manillas: large rings of brass traded by the Europeans for Benin goods

mudfish: fish with primitive lungs that allow it to survive on land for brief periods during the dry season in West Africa. Its ability to survive in two worlds is likened to the double nature of the *oba,* who is both human and godlike. A symbol of kingship.

oba (OH-bah)**:** godlike ruler of Benin, believed to be descended from the son of a god and thought to control the forces that determine the kingdom's well-being

Obieve (oh-bee-AY-vay)**:** daughter of **Osanobua**; goddess of childbirth and agriculture

ododo (oh-DOE-doe) **cloth:** red cloth like flannel. Because its color is like the skin of a scaly anteater, which can sometimes defeat a leopard, this cloth symbolizes hidden strength. It is worn by Edo chiefs during ceremonies.

ogiso (oh-gee-SO)**:** "ruler of the sky"; title held by the first hereditary chiefs of Benin, who ruled before the kingdom came under the control of one powerful leader, the *oba*

Ogiuwu (oh-gee-OOH-woo)**:** son of **Osanobua**; god of death

Ogun (oh-GOON)**:** god of iron; patron of smiths, hunters, and warriors; in modern times, patron of taxi drivers and metalworkers

Olokun (OH-low-koon)**:** son of **Osanobua**; god of the sea

Osanobua (oh-san-oh-BOO-ah)**:** the supreme god. He divided the earth among his three children.

palace chiefs: chiefs responsible for the care of the *oba* and his palaces; derived most of their power from their closeness to the *oba*

renaissance: a renewal or rebirth

ritual: a ceremony or act, usually religious, in which several steps are followed very carefully

town chiefs: chiefs responsible for administering one or several Benin territories and for being the middlemen between the *oba* and the villages

Ugie Erha Oba: annual festival that honors the *oba*'s father and his paternal ancestors

uzama (ooh-ZAH-mah)**:** nobles who are the highest-ranking chiefs in Benin. Unlike the other chiefs, their titles pass from father to son. They are considered descendants of the chiefs who requested a new ruler to found the current royal dynasty.

FOR FURTHER READING

Anderson, David A. *The Origin of Life on Earth: An African Creation Myth*. Mount Airy, Maryland: Sights Productions, 1991.

Barker, Carol. *An Oba of Benin*. London: MacDonald and Jane's, 1976.

Bryan, Ashley. *The Ox of the Wonderful Horns and Other African Folktales*. New York: Atheneum, 1993.

Equiano, Olandah; adapted by Anne Cameron. *The Kidnapped Prince: The Life of Olandah Equiano*. New York: Knopf, 1995.

Haskins, James. *Black Dance in America*. New York: HarperCollins, 1990.

Haskins, James. *Black Music in America*. New York: Harper-Collins, 1987.

Hoobler, Dorothy, and Thomas Hoobler. *The African American Family Album*. New York and Oxford: Oxford University Press, 1994.

Ibazebo, Isineme. *Exploration into Africa*. New York: New Discovery Books Macmillan, 1994.

Lester, Julius. *Black Folktales*. New York: Grove Press, 1991.

Murray, Jocelyn, ed. *Africa: Cultural Atlas for Young People*. New York: Facts on File, 1990.

BIBLIOGRAPHY

Barker, Carol. *An Oba of Benin*. London: MacDonald and Jane's, 1976.

Boahen, Adue, with J. F. Ade Ajayi and Michael Tidy. *Topics in West African History*. Harlow, Essex: Longman, 1986.

Bradbury, R. E. *The Benin Kingdom and Edo-Speaking Peoples of Southwest Nigeria*. London: International African Institute, 1964.

Bradbury, R. E. *Benin Studies.* London: Oxford University Press, 1973.

Conton, W. F. *West Africa in History,* vol. 2, *Since 1800.* London: George Allen & Unwin, 1966.

Darling, P. J. *Archaeology and History in Southern Nigeria: The Ancient Linear Earthworks of Benin and Ishan.* Cambridge: Cambridge Monographs in African Archaeology 11, 1984.

Davidson, Basil. *Africa in History—Themes and Outlines.* New York: Collier, 1968.

Davidson, Basil. *The African Genius: An Introduction to African Social and Cultural History.* Boston: Atlantic Monthly Press, 1969.

Davidson, Basil. *A History of West Africa to the Nineteenth Century.* Garden City: Anchor Books, 1966.

Egharevba, Jacob B. *A Short History of Benin.* Ibadan, Nigeria: Ibadan University Press, 1968.

Ezra, Kate. *Royal Art of Benin: The Perls Collection.* New York: The Metropolitan Museum of Art, 1992.

Fagg, William. *Divine Kingship in Africa.* London: The Trustees of the British Museum, 1978.

Gallembo, Phyllis. *Divine Inspiration: From Benin to Bahia.* Albuquerque: University of New Mexico Press, 1993.

Home, Robert. *City of Blood Revisited: A New Look at the Benin Expedition of 1897.* London: Rex Collings, 1982.

Murray, Jocelyn, ed. *Cultural Atlas of Africa.* New York: Facts On File, 1981.

Oliver, Roland, ed. *The Dawn of African History.* London: Oxford University Press, 1968.

The Royal Art of Benin: A Resource for Educators. New York: The Metropolitan Museum of Art, 1994.

Thompson, Robert Farris. *Flash of the Spirit: African and Afro-American Art and Philosophy.* New York: Vintage Books, 1984.

INDEX

Page numbers for illustrations are in boldface

ABOUT THE AUTHOR

Heather Millar grew up in San Francisco and attended Stanford University, where she studied world history and Chinese language. After graduating she spent eighteen months studying Chinese at Peking University in the People's Republic of China. She enjoys writing about historical subjects as well as about current affairs. She has contributed articles to the *New York Times, Business Week,* and *The Atlantic Monthly.* She is the author of another title in Marshall Cavendish's Cultures of the Past series: *China's Tang Dynasty* (1996).

Heather lives in New York City with her husband, Peter, a newspaper editor, and her stepdaughter, Maureen.

DATE DUE